HOUSMAN'S PLACES

To Kate

HOUSMAN'S
Places

Robin Shaw

The Housman Society
Bromsgrove

First published in the United Kingdom by The Housman Society, 80 New Road, Bromsgrove, Worcestershire, B60 2LA

ISBN 0 904579 03 4 Paperback
ISBN 0 904579 04 2 Hardback

British Library Cataloguing-in-Publication Data
A catalogue record for this book is available from the British Library

Designed by Geoff Green, Swavesey, Cambridge.
Typeset in Palatino
Origination by Sadler Print, Stourbridge.
Printed in the Great Britain by Ebenezer Baylis & Son Limited, Worcester.

Contents

Introduction

The literary pilgrim

'I did not apprehend that the faithful would be making pilgrimages to these holy places', wrote A. E. Housman when his brother, Laurence, gently chided him with romantic falsification in attributing a steeple to Hughley church when there is none. Well, literary pilgrims are around in increasing numbers, as for example, a visit to Haworth or Dove Cottage will quickly confirm.

Why do we do it? There are the purists who insist that authors' works should stand complete on their own merits without explanation or supplementary information. Housman himself said, 'The centre of interest in a poet is his poetry: not his themes, his doctrines, his opinions, his life or conduct.' But most of us cannot leave it at that. We like to know more about the author, what influenced him and led to his works, and, where an artist has evoked a feeling for a place, we want to know that place. We become pilgrims and this is a book for literary pilgrims.

Housman achieved excellence as a classicist and a poet. A few people understand his contribution to Latin and Greek scholarship and I would be pleased if they joined the ranks of the pilgrims, but this book is put together primarily for those who are lovers of Housman's poetry. If the reader already knows Housman's work well or has read much about him, I hope it will enhance his or her pleasure. There is not a great deal in this book that has not been published before, but it is intended to bring together information in a useful form.

For those readers who know Housman less well, hopefully it will lead to greater involvement and pleasure from his works.

There is a third category; the readers who know little of Housman's works. For these perhaps there will be some delight of discovery. As I have researched the places for the book, it has become increasingly apparent to me that by following in Housman's footsteps a visitor to Britain would be exposed to a selection of some of the finest that England has to offer in landscape, architecture, and history.

I have tried to gather together information which will help to conjure up the past. If you believe in ghosts, and who does not, at least to the extent that the imagination can paint pictures of people of the past, then about the lanes of Fockbury, through Hampstead Heath and Highgate Woods, through flat fields round Cambridge, there you can glimpse a dapper, slight, trim figure of a man, cane in hand, walking briskly and purposefully, rarely pausing, looking straight ahead. As he passes you, his face looks kindly enough, but you may be disturbed by the sadness in his eyes. And if you speak, he will imperceptibly stiffen in anger and ignore you. He is alone with his thoughts and does not want to be disturbed. You have glimpsed A. E. Housman, walking, as he did for relaxation throughout his life. The purpose of this book is to help you get such glimpses.

Although Housman was a classical

scholar, it was his poetry that made his popular reputation. With just a few words at a time he evokes a whole landscape and conveys deep emotional themes. It was from his sadness that the poems welled up inside him and it was his scholarship that allowed such perfect expression.

He chose Shropshire as the setting for his poems. The enigma is that he never lived there and his visits were few. I hope that no one will be disillusioned or put off his poetry by this truth or discouraged from visiting Shropshire, accompanied by *Collected Poems*. Shropshire stirred Housman's imagination and he captured an aspect of its spirit to such an extent that his poems have been taken to the hearts of Shropshire people. So while Shropshire is very much a part of this book, mostly it covers the places where he actually lived or frequently visited - Bromsgrove in Worcestershire, Oxford, London, Cambridge and Woodchester.

The book is about Alfred Edward Housman. Through it I have mostly referred to him by his initials, A.E.H., for that is how he was known to friends and that is how he signed letters even to his dearly loved step-mother. Only when referring to him as a child, and to distinguish him from other members of the family, have I taken the liberty of referring to him as Alfred.

Other members of the Housman family appear in the biographical material as and when they are particularly relevant. There were some very interesting and talented members of the family but every undertaking must have its limits.

The Form of the Book

The literary explorer of places goes seeking the past with the imagination finely tuned. It needs to be, for places today are not what they were. Sometimes they have been cleaned up, painted and 'improved' out of all recognition. Sometimes motorways have been driven through and seclusion lost. The text and photographs and maps and drawings have been selected to feed the process of discovery.

This is a guide to places, rather than a biography. It is not really intended for straight-through reading. The main text covers relevant biography, descriptions of places and buildings and historical background. Each section is designed to be complete in itself and this leads to a degree of repetition across sections which can be tedious if they are read in quick succession. I have tried to keep repetition to a minimum but would rather err in ensuring self-sufficiency in each section than the reverse.

The sequence of places covered is broadly chronological, as they were important in A.E.H.'s life. This does, therefore, if you read it straight through, lead to a kind of biography and there is a reasonable progression through the book. Reasonable, but not complete for several reasons. In the Bromsgrove section the story is complicated by the fact that the family moved back and forth between residences. A.E.H. was born in the Valley House, spent his first twelve years at Perry Hall, then moved to the Clock House until he left for university. After that the family returned to Perry Hall, so A.E.H. was there for vacations and for some months between coming down from Oxford and starting at the Patent Office.

Then there is Woodchester which A.E.H. visited all through his life. I have given Woodchester penultimate position.

And there is Shropshire, where A.E.H. never lived but which was the inspiration for his poetry. I have reserved Shropshire until last; which is appropriate, for that is where his memory most strongly lives.

To help cross-referencing, a name in bold type indicates that it is the subject of significant separate references in the book and there is a simple index to places and people at the back of the book.

The annotations in italic type give information on exactly what there is to see now, and specific data on opening arrangements, accessibility, etc.. Every effort has been made to see that this is accurate at the time of going to print, but inevitably things will change. The publishers will be grateful if you let them know of such discrepancies or errors.

Housman lived in and was associated with some very beautiful and interesting places. This book cannot be a full guide to those places and is largely confined to what is relevant to A.E.H.. While you are on the spot you will no doubt want to see other things and a few pointers are given on sources of information.

Even on A.E.H., I cannot claim that the book is more than an introduction. Fortunately there are excellent biographies in print or recent enough to be available in many libraries and for further reading a brief bibliography is placed at the end.

A.E.H's poems were originally published in four volumes; *A Shropshire Lad* and *Last Poems* during A.E.H.'s lifetime, and *More Poems* and *Additional Poems* after his death. Often they are now combined as sections within one volume of *Collected Poems*. The following abbreviations are used when referring to these.

ASL *A Shropshire Lad*
LP *Last Poems*
MP *More Poems*
AP *Additional Poems*

Most editions number the poems in Roman numerals.

Poems are printed wholly or in part in this book when they are arguably biographical or very relevant but a collected edition of the poems is really an essential accompaniment to a pilgrimage.

A. E. Housman

A drawing by Francis Dodd
commissioned by St John's College,
Oxford in 1925 when A.E.H. was 66

A. E. Housman

A. E. Housman was first and foremost a classical scholar - that was, he said, his trade. He devoted his life to Latin and Greek and specialised in a branch of scholarship known as textual criticism.

The texts of the work of ancient authors seldom come down to us in one definitive version. In antiquity scribes copied out the manuscripts, one from another, over decades and centuries. They made mistakes and changes and it is as if a long game of Chinese whispers took place, so that we end in modern times with a variety of differing texts. The textual critic examines these with a view to determining what the author first wrote and intended. He needs to have a very good knowledge of the language concerned and its usage at the time. He needs to examine the various texts to form a view on their date and claim to authenticity and to compare them in detail. He needs to know the work of the author so thoroughly that he can, so to speak, get inside his mind and judge what it is likely he would have said; to recognise his 'voice'. It is a discipline which calls for a very keen intellect and long hours of concentrated study. The outcome is a text of the author which the textual critic believes is as close to what the author wrote as is possible to establish.

Where he feels it necessary the textual critic will 'emend' an existing text and publish a new text supported by his notes on how this has been arrived at.

A.E.H. devoted himself to this work leading a disciplined and lonely life. He lived in the mind with Greek and Latin writers and poets. As time went on he concentrated on Latin because he was given appointments in Latin rather than Greek, but he was at the forefront of scholarship in both.

The disciplines of his academic calling permeated his whole life. He sought truth and accuracy. Accuracy was not a virtue , he said, but a duty, and while he struggled to interpret the mistakes of scribes of old he scourged compositors who got the punctuation of his articles and poems wrong.

What kind of a man was he? He was dry and shy and reserved. He repelled strangers and would pass by his friends in the street. He had a caustic tongue which had no mercy on those he did not agree with or whom he felt fell short of the standards which were expected of them. He was deeply sensitive and we shall see that a recurring theme of his poems was the impossibility of coming to terms with 'a world he never made'. He was a scourge to anyone who claimed to be an expert and appeared to fall short on expertise.

And yet he was a man of humour. All his life he wrote comic verse for the amusement of friends and he was much in demand as an after dinner speaker. Unfortunately little has survived to tell us what he said but his facility with words coupled with his dry delivery must have been a winning combination.

So a scholar and a poet and a wit

he became. What of his origins? He was born in Fockbury, nearly two miles from Bromsgrove in Worcestershire in 1859. He was born into a family which had the lifestyle of the middle class of his day. It meant living in the big houses of their community: it meant the expectation of going into professions, mainly the church and the law: it meant cooks, maids, gardeners and governesses; and it meant horses and carriages. The Housmans were such a family; there was enough wealth to give a sense of security and to buffer those of the family who were inadequate from the vagaries of the world. They were conservative in politics and Church of England in religion, involved in their communities, carrying the burdens of the community as was expected of the local gentry, the backbone of town and parish committees; if not vicars, then church wardens.

In such families some individuals in their time add to the stock of family wealth and others draw upon it. Edward Housman, A.E.H.'s father, was one who drew. He drew his share and he drew beyond it. He ensured that nothing was passed on to his children. All this is covered later; sufficient here to say that when Alfred was in his early childhood security seemed absolute. If his father did not prosper then his grandmother was wealthy and such families did not go under. Alfred grew up with his brothers and sisters in Perry Hall, Bromsgrove, enjoying a perfect childhood, and won a scholarship to Bromsgrove School where he received an excellent classical grounding.

The death of his much-loved mother when he was twelve brought the perfect childhood to a sudden stop. Traumatically, it brought trouble into his life and disillusion with religion. Alfred never recovered his faith and from then on his guard was up against whatever life had to offer.

Gradually family life was resumed. Edward married again, to his cousin, Lucy from Woodchester and the family moved to the Clock House where Edward had been brought up, a large house in the country with an estate of farms and cottages. Some good years followed when the family, though struggling financially, enjoyed rural life.

Alfred won a scholarship to St. John's College, Oxford. He went there in 1877 full of confidence; carrying the hopes of his family. For most of his four years all seemed well; success seemed assured - and then he failed his final examinations. How could this happen to one who had such ability? A.E.H. never explained but two key points are, that concentrating on texts of Propertius and disapproving of the Oxford 'Greats' syllabus, he did not read all the books he should have read, and that he fell in love with a fellow student, Moses Jackson.

The family were now in dire straits with Edward ill and penniless. Alfred was faced with the necessity of earning a living. He studied at home for the civil service examinations, and spent one further term at Oxford to qualify for a pass degree. He got a job as clerk in the Patent Office in London where Moses Jackson was employed.

For ten years he worked there, 'in

the gutter' he said, and then he applied for and was accepted as Professor of Latin at University College London. The key to this remarkable transition was his determination to be recognised as a scholar. He had, unknown to colleagues in the Patent Office, studied and published classical papers that had attracted the attention of the leading classical scholars of his time.

In his early years at University College London he wrote the poems which went into *A Shropshire Lad*. They were born out of the troubles he had suffered in life - the death of his mother, failure at Oxford, coming to understand his homosexuality and the impossibility of being open about it, rejection by Moses Jackson and the death of Adalbert Jackson, and the family financial problems and the death of his father.

After rejections by several other publishers, he paid for *A Shropshire Lad* to be published by Kegan Paul, Trench, Trubner & Co. Ltd.. When it appeared his family were astonished, and so were his colleagues at University College. He was not as austere and unfeeling as he seemed. Nevertheless the two sides of his life as poet and scholar were kept apart and his colleagues knew better than to try to talk to him about his poetry. The first edition sold slowly, and then Grant Richards, who was starting up as a publisher, persuaded A.E.H. to let him publish the poems. *A Shropshire Lad* was never out of print after that and his reputation as a poet steadily grew.

Meanwhile he continued as a classical scholar publishing many papers and beginning his great work, a five volume edition of the text of Manilius. A.E.H. spent nineteen years at University College London. In 1911 he applied for the position of Kennedy Professor of Latin at Cambridge University. He obtained this and became a fellow of Trinity College. He had achieved the highest level of scholarship and found a haven where he was recognised and could pursue his textual studies, building his classical monument of scholarship. He only produced one more slim volume of poems in his lifetime; *Last Poems* in 1922, published by Grant Richards.

He remained at Trinity College, Cambridge for the rest of his life. He lived the life of a college don, often taciturn and unapproachable. Daily, with total predictability in timing, he went from working in his rooms to meals in the college. He took a long walk every afternoon. He gave the few lectures that were demanded of him, eruditely and precisely, delivering them with scant awareness of his audience. Annually he went abroad in the summer, often to France where he enjoyed good food and vintage wines, and each year he spent time with his friends at Woodchester, with Percy Withers in Oxfordshire and with his brother, Basil, in Bromsgrove.

He finished his work on Manilius in 1930. He died in a Cambridge nursing home in 1936, aged 77.

Sidemoor Mill -
Benjamin Sander's Button Factory

Willow Road

Mr Sander's Gardener lived here

The National School

Crow - formerly

Hern and Trumpel

Parson's Hill

Clegg or Dipp

Kidderminster Road

The Vicarage

time Perry of the Hall A.E. Housman

St. John's House

The Heralds Mansion

Parish Church of St. John

Steps House

St. John Street

Roundabout House

Town Hall

The Old George

Little Lane

The Mount Pig and Pheasant

Worcester Street

Station - The Merch

The Old Fairground

Spadesbourne Brook

Hanover Street

The Black Cross

The Old Bar

or Dye ks

Worcester Road

Anno Domini House

Hill Lane

The New Black Cross or The Black and White Inn

Bromsgrove School
- refounded 1695 by Thomas Cokes -

Stalls

Dr. Collis's Bathroom

Dr. Collis's Tunnel

Kitelass Alley

Bromsgrove

Housman's Home Town

A.E.H. was born in 1859 at Fockbury, near Bromsgrove, lived at Perry Hall in Bromsgrove town until he was twelve, and then in the Clock House, Fockbury, until he went to St. John's College, Oxford in 1877.

Bromsgrove lies in north Worcestershire where the hills that fringe the Birmingham plateau at Clent, Romsley, Lickey and Cofton, gently subside to the Severn Plain. In Roman times a track, a saltway, ran north from saltworkings at Droitwich. Here, where Bromsgrove lies, it passed the knoll on which Bromsgrove's church, **St John's**, now stands and it ran alongside a brook that flowed from the Lickeys, the Spadesbourne. This was a natural place for settlement and a town grew from mediaeval times.

When A.E.H. was a boy in the 1860s and 70s, Bromsgrove was a market town of about 5000 people, serving a parish of 10,000 and an even larger rural hinterland. Its houses, workshops, pubs, coaching inns, shops and mills were clustered beneath the church and beside the long, straight High Street that the saltway had become. In those days of slower transport and smaller populations we have to envisage a town much more self-contained than today. Its people would mostly belong to the town, with ancestors going back for generations. The town was not isolated however; it was on the highway which ran from Bristol to Birmingham. Coaches regularly came up the High Street, changing their horses for the last lap, as the road ascended the Lickeys. In Housman's day coaching was already in decline; the railway had come to the town in 1840. From the High Street, by the Golden Cross Hotel, a horse-drawn bus shuttled to the station which was a mile and a half out of town.

The town's main function was as a trading centre and there was a street market every Tuesday, where farmers came in to sell produce and buy their needs. On market days the town would be busy and the pubs, of which there were many, did good business. On other days it was a quiet town, except at fairtime. Bromsgrove had long been famous for its fairs. The Midsummer Fair was an attraction for horse dealers from all over the Midlands and the country people would look forward to it for months.

The town also had industries, the most important of which was nail-making. In small brick workshops, in and around Bromsgrove, hundreds of people, working at forges, hammered

The southern end of Bromsgrove town about 1880
A reconstruction researched by Dr Alan Richards and drawn by Mr Norman Neasom for the Bromsgrove Society. Showing Perry Hall near the top left hand corner and many other places associated with the Housman family - St. John's, the Shoulder of Mutton, the fairground, John Adam's indigo factory and Bromsgrove School

out hand-made nails. This industry was dying in the late nineteenth century because of the competition from machine-made nails, and the nailers went out on extended strikes.

Other industries were cloth making, button making and there were numerous small crafts.

Bromsgrove's oldest and most impressive building was, and still is, **St John's Church** which was the focal point of the town. Beneath it the turnpike road from the west, the Kidderminster Road, entered the town. This would have been to modern eyes a country lane which ran between **Perry Hall** and the church.

Perry Hall was one of the largest houses on the fringe of the town. Set in its extensive gardens it provided a quiet haven for the Housman family, but the town began just outside their gates. Hanover Street and St. John Street were narrower than they are today and crammed with buildings. The Spadesbourne brook ran beneath a small bridge in Hanover Street and on past the fairground, which was where Watt Close is now. It continued passing John Adam's indigo factory and on to the large Cotton Mill which was powered by water from the Cotton Pool, stretching behind Perry Hall, over much of what is now Sanders Park.

As today, the High Street extended north from the crowded area where the current market building stands. The core of the old market was held at the southern end of the High Street, under the arches of the old town hall, long demolished, which stood where George House is now. The stalls and people surged out from there up the High Street, every house and shop having the right to sell goods on the pitch in front of it. From Georgian times brick had come to predominate in the architecture of the town, often concealing the timbering of buildings which were much older than they seemed.

A.E.H. was brought up with the town literally on his doorstep. He would experience the activities of rural town life with its quiet days, its

Bromsgrove horse fair - about 1910

HIGH STREET BROMSGROVE.

markets and fairs, with their noise and bustle, its coarseness and its human dramas. He would see the poverty of the nailers and the poor, uneducated children playing in the streets. Not surprisingly fairs feature in a number of his poems. All country life was just outside the gates of Perry Hall.

Bromsgrove about 1890
Looking south to the old town hall and market

When first my way to fair I took
 Few pence in purse had I,
And long I used to stand and look
 At things I could not buy.
                    From LP XXXV

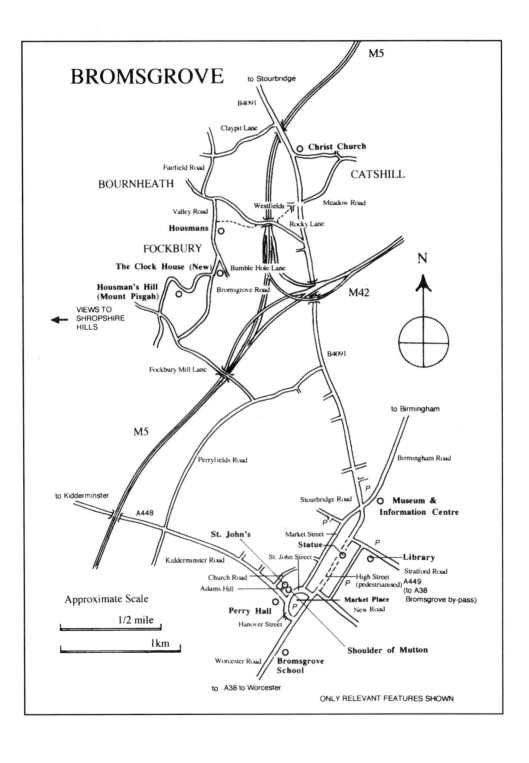

BROMSGROVE

to Stourbridge

M5

B4091

Claypit Lane

Christ Church

Fairfield Road

CATSHILL

BOURNHEATH

Meadow Road

Valley Road

Westfields

Housmans

Rocky Lane

FOCKBURY

The Clock House (New)

Bumble Hole Lane

Housman's Hill
(Mount Pisgah)

Bromsgrove Road

M42

VIEWS TO
SHROPSHIRE
HILLS

N

B4091

Fockbury Mill Lane

to Birmingham

M5

Birmingham Road

Perryfields Road

P

to Kidderminster

Stourbridge Road

Museum &
Information Centre

A448

P

St. John's

Market Street

P

Statue

Library

St. John Street

Stratford Road

Kidderminster Road

Church Road

High Street
(pedestrianised)

A449
(to A38
Bromsgrove by-pass)

Adams Hill

P

Perry Hall

P

Market Place

New Road

Approximate Scale

Hanover Street

Shoulder of Mutton

1/2 mile

1km

Worcester Road

Bromsgrove
School

to .A38 to Worcester

ONLY RELEVANT FEATURES SHOWN

Bromsgrove now

* Bromsgrove is situated 12 miles south-west of Birmingham. It is most easily reached by road being near where the M42 meets the M5. There are buses from Birmingham and some trains but the station is a mile and a half out of the town.

* Bromsgrove is now surrounded with overspill housing and the motorway network but its town centre is pleasantly pedestrianised, which shows off to advantage the architecture of its modest buildings. It takes a little imagination to see the town as it was with the traffic of horse-drawn coaches coming up the High Street. Although half the buildings have been charmlessly rebuilt or reconstructed since the 50s, the fact that they retain the old building line ensures that the general character of the town is unchanged. It is much brighter,with modern shop signs and paintwork, than it would have been in the nineteenth century, when paintwork would at best have been dull and country dust or mud would be well distributed. The older buildings have facades of a variety of periods, mostly Georgian and Victorian but some much earlier. Brick predominates but there is some timber-framing and sandstone. The general effect is good.

* Around today's market hall, there has been most change. The area which is now a car park, beside St John Street was heavily built up in earlier days with cottages, workshops and public houses.

* Beside Market Street, where there is now a large supermarket and car park, there was the cattle market.

* In and around the town, there are various places of direct Housman interest. The most important are **Perry Hall,** now an hotel, **Bromsgrove School** and **St John's Church** . These are covered later.

* **The Shoulder of Mutton** public house in St John Street, just round the corner from Perry Hall, is Victorian beneath its weatherboard and paint. This building replaced a very old coaching inn. In the nineteenth century it was a favourite hostelry for adjourning to after parish meetings. A.E.H.'s father, Edward, would have been included. The landlord also supplied beer and sherry to Perry Hall and Edward Housman signalled for extra supplies by throwing stones on the tin roof of an outbuilding of Perry Hall.

* At the lower end of the High Street on the right is the Golden Cross Hotel. The thirties building, in which it has survived, replaced another old coaching inn where much parish and town business was done and where Edward Housman was a regular customer.

* A.E.H.'s statue stands in the top half of the High Street, facing Lloyds Bank, a fine Georgian building.

High on a pedestal A.E.H. stands, pensive, cap and stick in hand, as when he went on the long walks which were his relaxation and exercise for most of his life. It was when walking that his poems came to him and the statue attempts to capture this. It was sculpted by Kenneth Potts and erected in 1985. The town owes the existence of the statue to the initiative of Joe Hunt and John Pugh who together founded the Housman Society in 1973. They organised the fundraising and commissioning, with considerable help from the District Council.

* A little further up the High Street on the right is Peacocks Stores, an attractive Georgian building. Here there was once a dame school said to have been attended by the Housman children.

* Round the corner at the top of the High Street on the right is the County Library. This has a collection of books about A.E.H. and the family. Some are for loan and others are for reference and can be viewed on request.

* Running north from the High Street is Birmingham Road and on the right is Bromsgrove Museum and Information Centre. From 1996 the Museum will have an exhibition about Housman and his connections with Bromsgrove. It also has a collection of exhibits from old Bromsgrove. The Information Centre has much general material about the area. Both are open Monday to Saturday, 9.30 to 5.00 and Sunday 2.00 to 5.00. The address is 26 Birmingham Road. Tel. 01527 831809

* *There is an official Housman Trail covering many of the Bromsgrove features in this book. It starts at the Market Place and is signed with brown finger posts. Catshill and Fockbury are two miles away so a car is recommended, though buses run from Bromsgrove through Catshill. Trail leaflets are available from the Museum and Information Centre (see above).*

Christ Church, Catshill - God's Acre

Here A.E.H.'s grandfather, the Rev Thomas Housman, was appointed curate in 1838 when the church was newly built, here A.E.H. was christened, and when living at Fockbury attended the church, and here are a number of the family graves.

Christ Church, Catshill, is the first stop on the official Bromsgrove Housman Trail and it is a good place to begin the Housman story.

The church, old beyond its years, its pink-red sandstone crumbling, sits on the Stourbridge Road, behind a sandstone wall, in a tree-shaded churchyard . It was built in 1838 as a chapel of ease within the Bromsgrove parish.

The Rev Thomas Housman arrived in Bromsgrove from Kinver, 10 miles away in Staffordshire, where he had been vicar for some years. The Housman family came originally from Lancaster, where Thomas's father, the Rev Robert Housman, the vicar of St Anne's Church, was a notable cleric - the calling of the church ran strongly in the Housman family. (St Anne's is now the Duke's Playhouse and a portrait of the Rev Robert Housman hangs in the Housman Gallery in the theatre.) Thomas was educated at Lancaster Grammar School and St John's College, Cambridge.

While at Kinver, he had a number of reasons for visiting Bromsgrove. His brother William had married a

Vernon of nearby **Hanbury Hall** and his uncle and good friend, John Adams, owned **Perry Hall**. Even more importantly he had met Ann Brettell of the **Clock House**, Fockbury. He married Ann in 1822 and they lived in Kinver until 1836.

A move to Bromsgrove was possibly prompted by a desire to be near Ann's ageing, widowed father, Joseph Brettell and in 1838 Thomas accepted an appointment as curate at St John the Baptist's Church. This was, however only the first step in a family plan and the Adams and Brettells were soon involved in a project to build a church for the people of Catshill, Bournheath and Fockbury.

While the church was being built the Housmans lived at Lydiate Ash but when Thomas took up the incumbency they moved into the Clock House to live with Ann's father and her sister, Mary Brettell. They took with them their five children.

Thomas was at first curate and then vicar of Catshill over a period of 26 years until 1864 when he retired. During that time Catshill became a parish in its own right with a few hundred people and a congregation made up of yeoman farmers, farm labourers and nailers. Laurence Housman, A.E.H.'s brother, later remembered the men coming to services on Sunday dressed in the clean smocks which they would then wear all week and he also remembered that some of them wore beaver hats which were fashionable at the time. Thomas is said to have been a man of powerful presence with a voice which made the congregation

Christ Church, Catshill
Old before its time

quake in their pews.

He had a reasonably large inherited fortune of his own and the Brettell family were wealthy, so the Housmans were established as a family of some substance in the Bromsgrove community. Thomas was important not only in his clerical capacity but also, although he never personally owned it, as the apparent master of the Fockbury estate. He played a strong role in public affairs and in general was the epitome of a country gentleman.

Thomas and Ann's family increased from five to seven. Edward, the second eldest, married Sarah Jane Williams of **Woodchester** and Alfred

Edward, their first born was christened at Christ Church on Easter Sunday 1859. This was an important and joyful family occasion. The Housman baby was christened together with the children of two nailers and those of a labourer and a groom of the parish. Many relatives gathered; aunts and uncles and a contingent from Woodchester which included Mrs Wise who was a godmother.

When Joseph Brettell died he left the estate to his daughter, Mary, and the Housman family continued to live with her. She died in 1867 leaving the Clock House to the Housman family. She is buried in Catshill churchyard.

Soon after Mary's death, Thomas and Ann retired completely and moved to Lyme Regis. They did not have long together in retirement; the Rev Thomas Housman died in 1870 and was buried in the Catshill churchyard. His grave is marked by a tall cross with the inscription, 'To whom was first entrusted this church, this God's acre.' A.E.H., a child of 10, was among the mourners.

The following year A.E.H.'s mother died and was buried in the family corner. A.E.H. was not at the funeral; he was away at Woodchester. His mother's grave gave the churchyard a feeling of desolation. A.E.H. wrote in later years:

God's Acre

Morning up the eastern stair
Marches, azuring the air,
And the foot of twilight still
Is stolen toward the western sill.
Blithe the maids go milking, blithe
Men in hayfields stone the scythe;
All the land's alive around
Except the churchyard's idle
    ground.
There's empty acres west and east,
But aye 'tis God's that bears the
    least:
This hopeless garden that they sow
With the seeds that never grow.

AP XI

After the Rev Thomas Housman's death, the Housman connection with Christ Church continued because his son, Edward brought his family to live in the Clock House from 1872. Edward married again, to his cousin Lucy. At this time he moved the seven chestnut trees he had first planted for each of his children at Perry Hall, to Catshill churchyard. For a few years A.E.H., from the age of 13, would be included in the family party walking the mile to church twice each Sunday. He would often pay a poignant visit to his mother's grave.

From 1877, when A.E.H. had gone to Oxford and Edward had moved the family back to Perry Hall, visits to Christ Church were on sad occasions. In 1881 the Rev Thomas Housman's wife died. A.E.H. was dutifully there, with the family, to see his grandmother buried with her husband. Now Edward learned that she had left the family wealth to other branches of the family.

In 1894 Edward Housman died and was buried here. Again A.E.H. mourned, returning from London where he was at **University College.**

The Rev Thomas Housman

The death of his father, despite all his father's faults, is one of the stresses to which A.E.H. was subject just before he was writing the poems in *A Shropshire Lad* .

Finally in 1907 A.E.H.'s stepmother Lucy, beloved Mamma, died in Hereford and was buried with Edward. This was the last family gathering at Christ Church. No doubt A.E.H. would visit the graveyard on his returns to Bromsgrove but any consistent Housman connection with Christ Church ended.

* *Christ Church, Catshill lies two miles out of Bromsgrove on Stourbridge Road, B4091 (signed Fairfield). It is on the right, half a mile after you pass under the motorway bridges. The church is locked except at service times. For access at other times contact the Vicarage, 403 Stourbridge Road, Catshill. Tel. 01527 8579619*

* *There are no relics of the Housmans inside the church. The font where A.E.H. was christened has been replaced.*

* *The family graves are in a group at the southern corner of the main church yard. Here lie:*

Thomas Housman, grandfather to A.E.H., and his wife Ann.

Edward Housman, father, together with Lucy Agnes, step mother and a daughter of the Rev Thomas Housman's brother William.

The family graves

Sarah Jane Housman (née Williams), mother.

Mary Brettell, great aunt.

Mary Theophania Vernon Housman, sister of Lucy Agnes.

* A number of the chestnut trees planted by Edward Housman to commemorate his children still exist and some of those that had died were replaced by the Housman Society in the 1970s.

* Near the church door there is a cherry tree. This is one of a number of trees donated by the Japanese branch of the Housman Society in 1976. Similar trees were also planted in Bromsgrove at Perry Hall and Bromsgrove School, and at St John's College, Oxford, University College London, and Trinity College , Cambridge.

* The fabric of the church - its soft sandstone eroding rapidly - is of serious concern. In 1994/95 the most needed repairs were carried out .

* When Edward Housman and his family of seven lived at the Clock House they used to walk to church twice a day on Sunday, Edward and Lucy in the lead. In pairs they walked, along Valley Road and across the fields to emerge at Stourbridge Road. There is still a part of the path which is signed as a footpath, off Westfields, a new housing development, opposite Meadow Road on Stourbridge Road. This section of pathway comes out on Rocky Lane by the Motorway bridge passing what were nailers' cottages. Enter it and you can easily imagine that Sunday ritual.

Housmans (The Valley House)

The birthplace of A.E.H., 26 March 1859

If you go looking for Fockbury, you will find no village. It lies just south of Bournheath, which does deserve the title of village for it has a good grouping of houses and several pubs. But Fockbury's farms and cottages are scattered. This piece of country, ancient enough to be mentioned in the Domesday book, owes its identity to having been included in the Fockbury estate, the farms and cottages belonging to the **Clock House.**

Housmans is a pleasing house with an early Georgian exterior. Deep within it are the timbers of a much older cottage, about which there have been developments and extensions, so that on the side facing the road there is a fairly straightforward facade, and away from the road there is an interesting assortment of roofs and gables. In earlier days it was a farmhouse. It was then known as the Valley House and was part of the Fockbury Estate.

It was here that Edward Housman, A.E.H's father, came to live with Sarah Jane Williams after they had married in **Woodchester,** near Stroud, in Gloucestershire in 1858. Sarah Jane was the daughter of the Rector of Woodchester, The Rev John Williams who was a classical scholar and a writer of poetry and hymns. The Williams family provided perhaps the strongest, though not the only, literary strain in A.E.H.'s ancestry.

Sarah was nearly 30 and Edward was 26. They settled happily into The Valley House which opportunely became free of tenants when they needed it. It was only a few hundred yards from Edward's parents in the Clock House and they could continue to enjoy the seclusion of the country and contact with the family. Edward was practising as a solicitor at **Perry Hall** and his sister was courting the farmer at Valley Farm, which is up the drive opposite Housmans.

A.E.H. must have been conceived on the couple's honeymoon as Sarah was immediately pregnant. She had a difficult pregnancy; for the birth her doctor came all the way from Wood-chester.

A.E.H. arrived on 26 March 1859. He was christened at **Christ Church**, Catshill - a happy family occasion.

He was not to live at the Valley House for long. Captain Adams of Perry Hall had died in 1858 and Edward was granted the life tenancy of the hall where he already had his offices. He decided to move the family in and did so three months after A.E.H. was born.

* To get to Housmans from Catshill Church by car first go back towards Bromsgrove for a third of a mile, turn right into Rocky Lane (signposted Bourn-heath), go over the motorway and at the junction veer left into Valley Road.

Or alternatively, following the official trail, continue on the Stourbridge Road away from Bromsgrove, over the

Edward Housman

Sarah Jane Housman (née Williams)

Housmans – A. E. H.'s birthplace

motorway and take the first turn left, Claypit Lane. Then left again and right into Valley Road.

* *In Valley Road, Housmans is 250 yards along on the left. It is now a private residence but it can be admired from the road.*

* *Valley Road too is little changed, except that in the mid-nineteenth century it would not be surfaced with tarmac. There are a few newer properties but it is still very rural. In Housman times there was a large yew on the opposite side of the road which reached right across the road nearly touching the windows of the house which was covered in creeper.*

The Site of the Clock House (Fockbury House)

The home of A.E.H.'s grand-mother, and family home to the Housmans from 1838 to 1878. Here A.E.H. lived in his teens.

The old Clock House, which was demolished by a developer in the early nineteen seventies, began as a 17th century manor house which was steadily engulfed with extensions and alterations. Probably the only 17th century element to be seen at the end was its tall chimneys. In Housman times it was already described as rambling. The original building would be half-timbered, but exten-sions were of brick and, after the Housmans sold it in 1880, it was extended again and given a full Victo-rian face-lift of mock timbering.

It was always a house of many gables and, before Housman times, in one gable there was a large clock and hence the house became known as the Clock House . Its even earlier name, and the one the Housman family used, was Fockbury House. (I will call it the Clock House here because that is what it was known by in the twentieth century.)

The gardens of the house were large, and well laid out with drives, paths and stone walls and were richly planted with trees. The total estate comprised several farms, including Valley House **(Housmans)**, Valley Farm and a number of cottages.

In the early nineteenth century the Clock House was owned and lived in by the Brettell family. Joseph Brettell was a solicitor as well as a landowner. The Rev. Thomas Housman, A.E.H.'s grandfather, married Joseph Brettell's daughter Ann and, when he became the incumbent at **Christ Church, Catshill** in 1838, just after the death of Joseph Brettell's wife, the family moved into The Clock House to live with Ann's father and her sister Mary.

Thomas and Ann lived there until the late 1860s. They arrived with a family of five and this grew to seven. The second eldest was Edward, who was later father to A.E.H.. Edward grew up like a young squire, enjoying country life, shooting and fishing. Fockbury, as we have seen, was very rural surrounded by fields, orchards, woods and close to a brook and a mill. Edward, as he grew older, trained as a solicitor, encouraged by his great uncle, John Adams, and he opened offices in the outbuildings of **Perry Hall**, John Adam's home. He left the Clock House to live in the **Valley House** when he was married in 1859.

The Rev Thomas Housman never owned the Clock House and its estate. Joseph Brettell died in 1847 and left the estate to his daughter Mary, who continued to live in the Clock House, together with the Housman family. From then on Thomas would appear to outsiders to be the master of the estate. He did not have a large parish and he had a curate to help him in the later years of his incumbency at Christ Church, so he was able to devote time to public affairs. He was a member of the Bromsgrove Board, the forerunner of the town council. He retired from the church in 1864 on

The Clock House

About 1860. This view is of the wing added by the Rev. Thomas Housman. He is in the garden with A.E.H.'s mother and A.E.H. as a baby

grounds of ill-health; he was 69. Three years later Mary Brettell died and left the estate jointly to Thomas and Ann's surviving children. Thomas and Ann retired to Lyme Regis. Thomas was not able to enjoy many years in retirement; he died in 1870.

For a time the house was tenanted, then Edward Housman, grieving for his lost wife Sarah Jane, and in financial trouble, moved the family from Perry Hall to the house he grew up in. It was not a move that made financial sense. He only had a fifth share in the Clock House and he alone would have to maintain it, as well as Perry Hall.

Thus it came about that A.E.H. spent some of his most impressionable teenage years at Fockbury. Just before the family moved to Fockbury he had been admitted to **Bromsgrove School** as a day boy. In term time he left home at seven in the morning to walk the mile and a half down into Bromsgrove, a long walk alone in quiet countryside.

Life at the Clock House was not easy. The facilities were rather spartan, no gas, no piped water and no drains, and with Edward in financial difficulties there were few servants. The children did not have their beloved Perry Hall garden but country life had much to offer.

Edward married again, to his cousin Lucy from **Woodchester**, who was quickly accepted as Mamma by the family. Alfred felt a responsibility, for his six brothers and sisters and when he was not at school or studying, found time to be their

The Clock House

A drawing of the 'restored' house in 1880 just after it had passed from the possession of the Housman family

leader and spent time with them reading and getting them to write and act in plays.

'The schoolroom at Fockbury in the holidays became the frequent scene of occupations of A.E.H.'s devising, mostly with some element of co-operation or competition in them. Drawing, painting, picture-making had their part, but plays and active games had a share, and above all he set us to work writing. We had to write "poems"; we had to write stories; and towards the end of his school days we had to contribute to a Family Magazine, that he wrote out himself in his small neat writing for annual circulation among relations and friends. We found great fun in all this, for Alfred had a way of making things he did amusing as well as interesting. Our gatherings were generally hilarious; yet in looking back, it is in these doings that we can now see that he had an emotional nature, subject to gloom that spread in spite of his efforts to subdue it.'

Katherine E. Symons, A.E.H.'s sister - from an article in The Bromsgrovian.

So it was never as carefree as it had been at Perry Hall before their mother died. Alfred's childhood contentment had gone along with his religion.

In 1877 Edward was deeper in financial trouble and was only able to afford one maid to help run the large house, and one horse for transport. He had mortgaged his share of the ownership of the Clock House and eventually he had to abandon any right to it at all. He was forced to move back to Perry Hall in 1878. That was the end of the Housman family's occupation.

The house was sold in 1880. Several families subsequently lived there but the one most remembered was the Morcoms. Colonel Morcom and his wife lived there from 1909 until the 1950s. They again extended and renovated the Clock House and Valley House, which they renamed Housmans.

A.E.H. returned for a last visit to the Clock House in 1935. He was staying with his brother Basil at the **Lower House**, Tardebigge and together they visited Catshill church fete which was held in the grounds of the Clock House by courtesy of the Morcoms.

*   *Along Valley Road, past Housmans, Bumble Hole Lane dives off to the left and a pair of houses form an arch. This is the gatehouse to what were the old Clock House grounds. A long brick wall marks the boundary to the end of Valley Road. Inside are two modern houses built in the seventies; one of these is the new Clock House. Behind them are the tall dark trees of the substantial gardens that accompanied the old house. There is a rich variety*

The last days of the Clock House

– as it was demolished to give way to the modern development

of mature trees, - a large cedar, some fine beeches and yews. There are some cherries too so A.E.H. could have been recalling Fockbury as well as Perry Hall when he wrote, 'Loveliest of trees,......, (ASL II I).

There is no public access to any of these grounds.

*   Rising over the wall alongside Valley Road is the ivy-covered clock tower which the Morcom family built in the 1920s restoring meaning to the name of the house.

*   There is a house at nearby Dodford which used to be called Fockbury Farm and is now called Fockbury House. This should not be confused with the house described above.

Housman's Hill - 'Mount Pisgah'

Views of the 'blue remembered hills, where A.E.H. was inspired by Shropshire.

There is a small hill just north of Bromsgrove, easily identified, because the B.B.C. has chosen to mark it with a large television mast, their unknowing monument to A.E.H.. The motorway planners too have ensured that it is noticed; it is at the end of the M42, where it joins the M5. This is a very special place to lovers of Housman's poetry. It is between Fockbury and Worms Ash, very close to the site of the old **Clock House** and after the move to Fockbury the Housman children often went up there. They named it 'Mount Pisgah', after the mountain which Moses climbed when leading the Israelites in their search for the Promised Land. It was an exciting place for children and it was one where Alfred would often go on his own. He particularly liked to meditate and watch the sun go down behind the Shropshire hills. He described this later in a poem.

> When summer's end is nighing
>   And skies at evening cloud,
> I muse on change and fortune
>   And all the feats I vowed
>   When I was young and proud.
>
> The weathercock at sunset
>   Would lose the slanted ray,
> And I would climb the beacon
>   That looked to Wales away
>   And saw the last of day.

From hill and cloud and heaven
  The hues of evening died;
Night welled through lane and
    hollow
  And hushed the countryside,
  But I had youth and pride.

And I with earth and nightfall
  In converse high would stand,
Late, till the west was ashen
  And darkness hard at hand,
  And the eye lost the land.

From LP XXXIX

The hill itself was not a place where beacon fires were lit but it was from here that the Housman family gathered together with some of the staff of Bromsgrove School to see the beacons lit for the Queen's jubilee in 1887. ASL I was the poem inspired by that occasion. The views from the hill are magnificent. The countryside drops down to the town of Bromsgrove. The tall church spire stands out as a marker for the part of town to where as a schoolboy A.E.H walked each day through dusty or muddy lanes and across the small-holdings and orchards of Sidemoor, alone and absorbing the country sights.

Beyond Bromsgrove the landscape opens to the Severn plain, flanked on on the one side by **Bredon** and on the other by Malvern, and a little nearer, to the south-west, the Abberley Hills. To the west the country rolls out to **Titterstone Clee** and **Brown Clee.** These views Alfred saw daily as he set off for school. He became intro-spective after his mother died but he found some consolation in this country and from the top of the hill, his imagination was particularly stirred and sadness settled on him.

> Into my heart an air that kills
>   From yon far country blows:
> What are those blue remembered
>   hills,
>   What spires, what farms are those?
>
> That is the land of lost content,
>   I see it shining plain,
> The happy highways where I went
>   And cannot come again.
>
> ASL XL

And so the distant Shropshire Hills where the sun went down, inspired the young man and the muse that brought forth 'A Shropshire Lad' first began to work.

* *I have called this hill, the children knew as Mount Pisgah, 'Housman's Hill'. Once you know of its significance you cannot fail to notice it as you drive on the M42/M5 interchange. Approaching Bromsgrove on the M42 from the west the television mast picks it out and beside it are the dark conifers of the mature trees of the Clock House gardens. In the distance are the Shropshire Hills.*

* *If you want to explore the area you can*

get there by car following the marked Housman trail. After **Housman's** and **the Clock House** in Valley Road, the signed trail carries straight on along Bromsgrove Road (very narrow) passing the old Clock House gardens.

* The field which tops the hill is private. To see the views without leaving the roads, you need to stop. It is best to park a car in Valley Road and walk. Follow the road veering to the right, rising and narrowing between sandstone banks and holly hedges. In 200 yards on the left are farm gates and the gate to the television station. From here you can see down over Bromsgrove and imagine the schoolboy's daily walk. Twenty yards further up the road are two gates on the right. From the second, weather permitting, you can see the Shropshire Hills.

* Housman's Hill is unnamed on modern Ordnance Survey maps. On very old ones it is Broom Hill. Its grid reference is 948729.

Housman's Hill
From the south with the dark trees of the Clock House gardens

Perry Hall

Home and office to A.E.H.'s father for much of the period from 1860 to 1894. This was the house in which A.E.H. enjoyed a happy childhood until he was twelve and his mother died.

The present Perry Hall was built by John Adams, uncle by marriage to the Rev Thomas Housman, A.E.H.'s grandfather. John Adams came to Bromsgrove in 1819 when he was 53. He was known as Captain Adams, though whether this was because he was a retired sea captain or because he was captain of Bromsgrove's military trained band is a matter of speculation. He bought an indigo dye factory in the ruins of an earlier Perry Hall but quickly decided to rebuild the factory on a site, not far away, by Worcester Road opposite Bromsgrove School. He then built a new house on the site of the old Perry Hall.

The Perry Hall he built is now an hotel. It has been considerably extended but the facade is much as when it was John Adams' home. It was a substantial house though the term hall was probably more appropriate for its predecessor. It has a good frontage made interesting by white neo-gothic windows and creeper-covered walls.

John Adams established himself in Bromsgrove society. He was not only a prominent factory owner but he was also the Distributor of Stamps for the area, a role which was akin to customs officer and necessitated Perry Hall being heavily protected with locks and shutters.

He was a good friend to his nephew, the Rev Thomas Housman, who was the vicar of Kinver and among his friends in Bromsgrove was Joseph Brettell of the **Clock House**, Fockbury, a landowner and solicitor whose daughter the Rev Thomas Housman married. John Adams was no doubt influential in establishing Thomas as the curate to the newly built **Christ Church, Catshill,** not long after Thomas had come to Bromsgrove.

John Adams remained close friends with the Housman family. When their son, Edward, became of age, he encouraged him to become a solicitor, set him up in offices in Perry Hall, gave him work that came his way and provided useful contacts.

When John Adams died Perry Hall was left jointly in trust for the children of Thomas and William Housman, i.e. Edward's brothers, sisters and cousins. Somehow the family were prevailed upon to allow Edward Housman to become a life tenant just after A.E.H. was born. Edward moved in during 1860 with his wife Sarah Jane and baby Alfred. Perry Hall was now both office and home and Edward lived there in style with a number of servants and in due course a governess for the children. He mortgaged land at Fockbury to pay for furniture.

There followed a number of very happy years. Brothers and sisters for Alfred appeared in quick succession - Robert, Clemence, Katherine, Basil, Laurence, and George Herbert - all by

1868.

    The house was later described by A.E.H.s sister, Kate, who became Mrs Symons.

'Inside the front door, on the east side of the house, there was a stone flagged hall, from which opened a number of large rooms, pleasantly furnished with some of the imposing Tudor and Queen Anne furniture which had come from Dr Williams' Rectory at Woodchester. There was a huge double kitchen, with two cellars, two coppers, a bread oven, two or three grinding mills, and a closed-up plate-warmer of enormous dimensions: and out in the yard, a beer cooler left over from the days of home brewing. Edward's small range of offices ran out from the north side towards Kidderminster Road, where the entrance to the property lay, and beyond which climbed the way to the church: a sloping path, with wide flights of steps, which had been built by John Adams and was therefore known as Adams' Hill.'

    As the family grew, Edward saw to his business as a solicitor and took part in public affairs. He was a father who ran a disciplined household, particularly with regard to religious observance, but he was a kindly

Perry Hall
– now an hotel

parent. Sarah Jane was also very pre-occupied with religion. She was inclined to high church within the Church of England, and would probably have changed to Roman Catholicism had it not been for the restraining influence of her husband. She had some of her father's bent for poetry and wrote skits on acquaintances.

Although there was much regulation in the household, the children found plenty of time to play and from the accounts of Alfred, Laurence and Kate we have a picture of idyllic childhood days. A.E.H. later said, 'Was there ever such an interesting family as we were'. The garden featured greatly in their lives.

'The garden was divided into three main sections: the ornamental, comprising lawns, flower-beds, and shrubbery; a well screened fruit and vegetable garden beyond; and to one side the 'rubbish garden' (our own name for it) which, having nothing in it of importance, was largely left to take care of itself. In it were two large apple-trees which bore a crop very sweet and small in kind, so numerous and negligible for dessert purposes that we took and ate them without a sense of sin. There were also damson-trees, exuding deliciously sticky gum, black currants, which in their raw state did not tempt us, and a 'clay hill' of which we made a fortress for our games, and thereon fought miniature battles. Recalling now those influences of early years, which formed so large a part of our education, for the shaping of character and the knitting of family relations, I doubt whether any were more valuable than that old garden, into which we plunged daily out of sight and sound of our elders, and there found liberty.'

Laurence Housman
The Unexpected Years

The idyll was broken when their mother became ill; she contracted breast cancer. Although this was the most serious problem for the family, it was not the only one; Edward's business was not prospering. He had never been very assiduous with regard to business: he had extended the house, the expense of running it was high, the children were coming up to the age when education could be expensive, and worrying about all this at the same time as his wife's illness, he took to drinking heavily, making matters worse.

After an illness of two years, Sarah Jane died on 26 March 1871. It was actually on Alfred's twelfth birthday. He had been sent away to stay with the Wise family in **Woodchester**. His father had felt, probably rightly, that as the oldest of the children he was the most devoted to his mother and the most vulnerable, and to be at home while she died would be too stressful. Alfred only returned after the funeral.

Edward was unable to meet the demands now made on him. Perry Hall was full of memories and sadness; he did something which seems irrational. **The Clock House,** which now belonged jointly to Edward and his brothers and sisters, became free of tenants and Edward decided to move back to the house in which he was brought up. He probably thought he would get a good rental by letting Perry Hall. In practice he ended trying to keep up two houses.

Alfred would be aware of these financial problems and together with grieving for his mother and observing his father's drinking, burdens were heavy upon him. It is fortunate that he was able to get a scholarship to **Bromsgrove School.**

The decline in fortunes continued and, while living at the Clock House, Edward nearly lost the right to Perry Hall. He had mortgaged it, in spite of the fact that it was held in trust for others of the family as well as himself. The mortgagee decided to call in the loan and in 1875 Perry Hall was sold at auction. Edward was already in litigation brought against him by other members of the family over his property machinations. He escaped from his latest problem by asking Edward Wise of **Woodchester** to buy Perry Hall at the auction, which he did acting as agent for Edward. The property was then remortgaged and Edward both wriggled out of his responsibilities to the other trustees and retained possession of the house. He was a tricky man to deal with.

But he was still committed to the repayments on the new mortgage. By 1878 Edward had to face reality; he had first mortgaged, and then lost any claim to his share of The Clock House and his brothers and sisters wanted him out. In any case he could not maintain two properties. Poorer,

Alfred aged seven (left) and his brother Robert in the garden at Perry Hall

and with reluctance, he moved the family back to Perry Hall, but at least this was a house they all loved.

That same year A.E.H. went up to **Oxford** and from then on was home at Perry Hall intermittently until he came back having failed his Finals. Then he was at home for some months while he studied for the civil service examinations and taught at **Bromsgrove School.** The family was very poor. Alfred's failure had been devastating to a family beset by many problems. The house was cold and Alfred worked on the dining table, contrite, introspective and uncommunicative but quietly determined to find a way forward.

After he left for London at the end of 1882, the family gradually dispersed. Edward and his second wife, Lucy, lived in Perry Hall, with financial help from relatives, until Edward died in 1894. Lucy stayed on until 1895. She then left for Hereford and lived there until she died in 1907. She was buried at Catshill beside Edward.

The Housman connection with Perry Hall ended.

* *Perry Hall is on the left, just as Kidderminster Road leaves Bromsgrove centre. It is an hotel owned by Jarvis Hotels. Its facilities are available to customers. Its telephone number is 01527 579976*

* *Inside the hotel there have been many alterations and redesigns over the years and it is difficult to discern what is original and what is not. Outside, the main facade is unchanged, even the front door is original. It has a square spy-hole which dates from John Adam's days when the property was very secure.*

* *The grounds are now largely car parks, secluded under yew trees. There are remnants of the walls of the old hall and with a little imagination you can recall the site with gardens and orchards where the children played.*

* *Cherry trees have always been a feature of Perry Hall. There was a large cherry at the front of the Hall in Housman's time, and there was a large cherry tree by the roadside until the nineteen-thirties. There is still a very large old cherry tree at the*
rear of the hotel. The age of this tree is uncertain but it is likely to be of the same stock as the trees of the old days.*

ASL II is probably A.E.H.'s best known poem and it is interesting to speculate about how it was inspired. Strictly it is about wild cherry trees but the presence of cherry trees at Perry Hall must have influenced A.E.H.

Loveliest of trees, the cherry now
Is hung with bloom along the
    bough,
And stands about the woodland
    ride
Wearing white for Eastertide.

Now, of my threescore years and
    ten,
Twenty will not come again,
And take from seventy springs a
    score,
It only leaves me fifty more.

And since to look at things in
    bloom
Fifty springs are little room,
About the woodlands I will go
To see the cherry hung with snow.

                                    ASL II

The Church of St John the Baptist

The family church to the Housmans of Perry Hall.

Viewed from from the southern end of Bromsgrove or from Perry Hall, St John's is dramatically elevated on a small hill ringed with lime trees. Its spire is its pride rising to nearly 200 feet. The church is built of red sandstone, essentially in perpendicular style with battlemented parapets and ornamented pinnacles.

As a result of its development over nine centuries those with an interest in architectural history can find many styles in its fabric and ornament. There was probably a Saxon church on the site and there was certainly a Norman one which was obliterated in successive rebuilding. The chancel is 13th century, there are substantial 14th century elements, and in 1858 Sir Gilbert Scott supervised a significant restoration which left the church with its present day appearance.

Prior to the nineteenth century St John's was the church to a very large parish indeed. It included Catshill and Fockbury.

Its place in the Housman story started when John Adams built Perry Hall in about 1824. No doubt he was a good churchgoer. He owned land on both sides of Kidderminster Road and to improve access to the church he built the flight of sandstone steps which gives easy access directly from **Perry Hall**. This side of the hill became known as 'Adams' Hill'.

The next connection with the Housmans came about when the Rev Thomas Housman, A.E.H.'s grandfather, was appointed to be curate of St John's for a short time until **Christ Church, Catshill** was built. He came in 1836 from being the vicar of Kinver but we must not assume that a curate's position was a demotion; at that time St John's did not have a vicar in residence in the town - it came directly under the authority of the Bishop of Worcester. In 1838 Thomas took up the incumbency at Catshill. It certainly looks as though he was then settling for a quiet life with less responsibilities in a small community on his wife's family estate.

Meanwhile John Adams continued to live in Perry Hall until a few years before his death in 1858. He was one of the first, if not the first, to be buried in the new cemetery which was being laid out to the west of the church.

Then Edward Housman came with his wife Sarah Jane and first child, A.E.H., to live in Perry Hall and the church became a very important element in the lives of their growing family. A.E.H.'s brother Laurence later wrote:

'For church-service, morning and evening, the bells rang a full half-hour; beginning small on two or three bells only, they mounted gradually to the full eight. The final crescendo took place at ten minutes to; this was our signal for a rush from happier engagements to get ready for church; and because it was a rush, we called them 'the dreadful bells', while in the scant time left, we got into our newest

St John's
'That spire whose serene beauty
was a presiding presence through
the years of our childhood......' -
Laurence Housman

pairs of boots (never shoes), brushed hair, washed hands, cleaned nails, and then for a finishing touch - boys as well as girls - put on gloves.

By the time the 'dreadful bells' had ended, we were all assembled with our governess in charge, ready to start. Last of all, at five minutes to the hour, came the 'ting-tang', a small cheerful wind-up on the treble bell; and as it began, forth we all sallied, crossed the road, went up the hill which was 'Adams Hill', and were in our places beautifully on time.'

(Laurence Housman – *The Unexpected Years*)

The children grew up under St John's, physically and spiritually, their lives regulated by its rhythms. They were not always reverential and Laurence recalled the boys attempting to use the weathercock on the spire for target practice with their air rifles.

So it continued until the death of Sarah Jane brought family life in Perry Hall to an abrupt end and Edward took the children to the **Clock House** for a few years.

Then they came back to Perry Hall in 1878. Edward was now married to his cousin, Lucy. A.E.H. was at **Oxford** and when he was home he joined the family at church even though he now privately declared himself an atheist.

In the remaining years until 1894 Edward lived at Perry Hall. While fit enough, he would climb the steps to join the congregation at St John's.

* *St John's stands as renovated by Sir Gilbert Scott while A.E.H. was a child. The lime trees which ring it are larger and it is difficult to look across to Fockbury as Alfred once did when he was away from home, convalescing from scarlet fever, and longing to be back with his stepmother, Lucy and his brothers and sisters.*

* *The church is locked when not in use. The Vicarage is on the right hand of the steps up Adam's Hill and visitors can apply for access. The address is 12 Kidderminster Road and the telephone number is 01527 876517*

* *The church publishes a brochure about the history and architecture of St John's.*

* *There is little to suggest the Housman connection inside the church. One of the panels in the organ screen carved by a local woodcarver, Robert Pancheri in 1970 depicts A.E.H. writing poetry on the bole of his favourite tree at Perry Hall. Inside the church on the east wall there is a memorial to the Bromsgrovians who died in the Boer War and Herbert Housman, A.E.H.'s brother, is listed.*

* *There is a memorial to John Adams in the cemetery across Church Street. It is in the centre of the island site down the main drive. There is no visible inscription.*

Bromsgrove School

Here from 1870 to 1877 A.E.H. received a good grounding in classics and won prizes for poetry.

To Edward Housman in Perry Hall the prospect of his family of seven approaching the age at which serious education was essential was a worrying one. Here was a man making ends meet by mortgaging property which was not strictly his; always on a financial knife-edge and yet at the same time having high aspirations and views about what was appropriate for a family of their standing.

Alfred and his younger brothers and sisters had been educated by a mixture of governesses and dame schools. In 1870 Alfred was 11 and a decision was necessary. It was very fortunate indeed that, a few hundred yards from Perry Hall, there was a good grammar school, about to be improved by a new headmaster, who would revitalise its system for scholarship places.

Bromsgrove School was founded in the fifteenth century as a grammar school for local boys and in 1693 it was substantially re-endowed by Sir Thomas Cookes. It was in and behind the building, now known as Cookes House, which faces onto Worcester Road. The lower part of this was built in 1695 and was a building of dignity and good proportion. It is still interesting but from an architectural point of view was not enhanced by the addition of an extra storey in 1859.

Here about seventy boys were taught by a headmaster and his staff. In 1868 there was a mixture of fee-paying day boys and boarders and a few 'Blue Coat' boys who were admitted free of charge. The endowment that supported the Blue Coat boys had dwindled and they were regarded as a burden and treated as inferiors. The new headmaster, Dr George Blore, changed all that. He established a system whereby there would be twelve foundation scholars who were day boys but in educational matters would be treated with total equality. They would only have to pay five pounds a year. It all happened just in time for Alfred. He passed the entrance test and was admitted as one of these foundation scholars in September 1870 at the age of eleven and a half.

The advent of the new headmaster was also fortunate for Alfred because Dr Blore was a classicist of considerable ability. While he did not teach Alfred himself, for Alfred had only risen to the fourth form when Blore left, he no doubt set the tone for classics teaching and Alfred was in an environment where his scholastic talent could develop.

He settled into school well. His sister, Kate, who became Mrs Katherine Symons, later recorded her memories of him at this time in a special edition of the school journal, The Bromsgrovian, published to commemorate his death.

'When A.E.H. began school he was a small quiet boy, solemn and studious. In his early days he was nicknamed Mouse, and boys would tread on him pretending they had not seen him. Quiet and studious he remained all his schooldays, yet by no means the sort of boy to be downtrodden. He had a determined personality, able to take his own way, and yet to avoid troubles. I cannot imagine his ever receiving punishment either at home or at school; and his life as a day boy ran with little room for oppression from school fellows.'

Dr Blore looking back said, that Housman was the sort of boy he was always afraid would ask him some question he could not answer.

As Alfred started at the school his mother was ill and dying. She spent

much time talking to him, treating him as an adult and encouraging him to feel responsibility for his younger brothers and sisters. She died in 1871 while Alfred was away at **Woodchester.** It was devastating for him and was as well that he had schoolwork to concentrate on.

Shortly after the death of his mother the family moved to the **Clock House,** Fockbury, giving Alfred nearly a two mile walk to school, and a very long day, but as we have already noted it was a time when he enjoyed being alone in the quiet of the countryside. There is a local story of how he liked to carry a vaulting pole, such as was popular with young people at the time, to amuse himself on the walk.

Dr Blore moved on and a new headmaster, Herbert Millington, came to Bromsgrove School. This was

The Old School House
– now known as Cookes House

another fortunate turn in A.E.H.'s life for Millington was an inspirational teacher of classics. He achieved remarkable successes for his pupils in scholarships and exhibitions to Oxford and Cambridge. He selected and trained staff well. Many of his masters became heads in their subsequent careers. He was interested in plants and gardens and he landscaped the school grounds and encouraged his pupils to take an interest in natural history.

By 1876 Alfred was in the sixth form and from then on received personal tuition from the headmaster. His addiction to Greek and Latin grew under Millington's enthusiastic direction. He received a prize at the end of the year, a volume of translations from English verse into Latin or Greek, *Sabrinae Corolla* edited by B. H. Kennedy, the headmaster of Shrewsbury School, which A.E.H. later said implanted in him a genuine liking for classics. (The Chair for Latin at **Cambridge** which A.E.H. eventually occupied was founded in honour of B. H. Kennedy.) A.E.H., was to remember Millington as being excellent for clever boys with a taste for classics but quite the reverse for other boys. There was no doubt about which category A.E.H. came into as a schoolboy .

Throughout his childhood, Alfred had written poetry and verse, humorous and serious, encouraged by his mother's example. At Bromsgrove School he took this seriously and, when fourteen, he entered a poem about Sir Walter Raleigh for the school verse competition. He did not win with this poem but later thought it better than some of his poems which did win prizes. He won prizes for verse in 1873, 1874 and 1875 and in his last year at Bromsgrove, 1877, won the Wattell Prize for greatest improvement in Latin and Greek and prizes for Latin and Greek verse. In his Oxford and Cambridge Leaving Certificate he gained distinctions in Latin, Greek, French and History.

He failed to win a scholarship to Corpus Christi College, Oxford but then won an open scholarship to **St John's College, Oxford** worth £100 a year. Millington, on his final school report, wrote 'May all my boys be like him!'

A.E.H. left to go to Oxford but that was not quite the end of the story of Bromsgrove School in A.E.H.'s life, for after failing Greats he came home to a family which was deeply in financial troubles. Then Millington proved a real friend and gave A.E.H. occasional employment teaching classics to the sixth form while he studied for a pass degree at Oxford and for the Civil Service examinations. In subsequent years Millington continued to watch over A.E.H.'s career and wrote a testimonial when he was applying to **University College London** for his first professorship.

While A.E.H. does not appear to have publicly expressed his gratitude to Bromsgrove School, there can be little doubt that it gave an environment where his own aptitude and industry could, with excellent guidance, enable him to leave as a very competent and confident young classicist.

Bromsgrove School today is a prosperous independent school for boarders and day pupils, boys and girls. It has nearly 1200 pupils. The grounds and buildings cover a large area to the south-east of the town with a main entrance off Worcester Road.

* From Perry Hall it is about three hundred yards walk to the old part of the school. In A.E.H.'s time this would be a walk across a small bridge over the Spadesbourne, passing clustering nailers' cottages and round into Worcester Road.

* The school buildings of A.E.H.'s time still exist. Twenty-five yards down Worcester Road you can see the basically, seventeenth-century School House, now known as Cookes House, facing down a slope behind a wall with large brick and stone gate posts.

It has a high, imposing facade. The additional storey, already added when A.E.H. was there, is easily detectable. It has beautifully panelled rooms on the ground floor , one of which is now used for the Governors' meetings. Behind it, in a wing forming an L shape, is the old headmaster's house and nearby in the Quadrangle Block are still the classrooms of the time which were then described as poor and dingy.

* Near these buildings is the Old Chapel, where A.E.H. attended school services, and between this and the modern staff centre are two cherry trees planted in Housman's memory. One is an English double cherry planted by Lord Cobham in the 1970s and the other is one of the Japanese trees given by the Japanese branch of the Housman Society in 1976.

* The landscaped school campus now extends far beyond the early buildings with many fine facilities. A building erected in 1913, known as Kyteless has a Latin inscription on its foundation stone the translation for which was supplied by A.E.H.

* The school has certain memorabilia and records of Housman including the special edition of the school magazine, 'The Bromsgrovian', referred to above, published in 1936 with recollections by Katherine Symons (sister), Laurence Housman (brother) and various academics who knew him well.

* While Cookes House can be seen from the public road, for access to the grounds and other enquiries you should apply to the Registrar, Bromsgrove School. Tel. 01527 579679.

Around Bromsgrove

The Lower House, Tardebigge, A.E.H.'s brother Basil's home.

In 1908 A.E.H.'s brother, Basil, a doctor, married Jeannie Dixon from Tardebigge. About 1910 they moved into the Dixon family home, the Lower House, with Jeannie's father, a widower. The Lower House is a large Victorian house, built in the 1850s, with gardens, orchards and a croquet lawn. They lived in a comfortable style largely as a result of the Dixon family wealth. Basil suffering from ill-health and, unable to run a general practice, was an assistant schools' medical officer.

When he was professor at **Cam-**

bridge a summer visit to Jeannie and Basil became part of the pattern of A.E.H.'s life. It is easy to imagine the pleasure of a few days in a comfortable family home as a change from spartan rooms in Cambridge. Basil and Jeannie had an old Austin car inherited from Jeannie's father. On his visits A.E.H. was taken on excursions and to venues for his walks such as Clent and Whitford by their chauffeur, George Smith. It was when staying here, with brother, Laurence, and sister, Clemence, that A.E.H. paid his last visit to the **Clock House.**

* The Lower House still exists as a private house. It is 2 $^1/_2$ miles east of Bromsgrove centre, map reference 990706.

Hanbury Hall, home of the Vernon family into which A.E.H's great uncle married.

Hanbury Hall, is a fine William and Mary-style, large, red-brick country house set in its estate. The Vernon connection first brought a member of the Housman family to Bromsgrove when William Housman married Mary Vernon (see **Christ Church, Catshill**). A.E.H's stepmother was a child of this marriage, a marriage which ended in **Woodchester** when William deserted his wife.

* Hanbury Hall is now owned by the National Trust. Whether A.E.H. ever went there is unrecorded. The link with him is rather loose but a visitor to Bromsgrove would enjoy going there. It is open April to October, Saturday, Sunday and Monday. 2.00pm to 6.00pm.

Clent Hills where A.E.H. walked.

In the hilly area north of Bromsgrove the highest summits belong to the Clent Hills. The views from there are magnificent in all directions. A.E.H. stood on Walton Hill, Clent from dusk to dawn on the night of Queen Victoria's diamond jubilee in 1897 and watched the beacons lit across the Midlands as he had done from **Fockbury** ten years earlier when he wrote ASL I. In later life he would walk on Clent when visiting the **Lower House.**

* The Clent Hills are 3 miles south-east of Stourbridge and five miles north of Bromsgrove, map reference 9379. They are owned largely by the National Trust and there is full access. They are still very good for walkers.

Oxford

Oxford and St John Baptist College

With every prospect promising, A.E.H. went up to St John's in the Autumn of 1877 but came away distraught in the summer of 1881.

When A.E.H. arrived in Oxford the old colleges were what they had already been for centuries, beautiful, grey stone buildings, serene beneath their spires, set in velvet lawns, clustering together in quiet dignity, and near at hand were meadows thick with wild flowers. Oxford was, however, developing fast and red-brick suburbia was spreading out northwards from St Giles, some of it houses for dons, newly permitted to marry and have families.

The Colleges, which had always been highly independent, and still are in many respects, were actively being integrated into the University, which is the entity which links the colleges and confers degrees. There was an air of change about.

A.E.H came at midsummer to take the scholarship examinations for St John Baptist College or St John's as it is usually known. He passed, was accepted and went up in October. He would travel by train from Birmingham, the line having opened in 1852, ending the era of horse-drawn coaches on that route, though horse transport still supplemented trains to London. The station was to the west of the city and horse-drawn omnibuses and Hansoms plied to the colleges.

St John's is situated at the northern edge of old Oxford to the east of St Giles, that broad area where the roads from Woodstock and Banbury converge, which has served for hundreds of years as an open space for events; the successor to the ancient fair still takes place there every September.

St John's was founded in 1555 by Sir Thomas White, based on a monastic college, St Bernard's, which did not survive the dissolution of the monasteries. The ancient gateway under the old statue of St Bernard is set in a building which dates from the founding of the College, though the dormer windows were added in 1662. It opens into the Front Quadrangle, the first of the two quadrangles which are formed by the older buildings of the College.

A.E.H. at eighteen

The Hall, which together with the Chapel, makes up the north side of the Front Quadrangle, is the ancient refectory of St Bernard's built in 1502. The Chapel was consecrated in monastic times but restored in 1843.

The Second or Canterbury Quadrangle was completed in 1636 in Renaissance style to honour King Charles I and has a statue of him at one end and a statue of Queen Henrietta Maria at the other. It was in the past attributed to Inigo Jones but this attribution is no longer supported. Nevertheless it is one of Oxford's finest architectural sights. The south and east sides are occupied by the Library. An archway goes through to several acres of very fine gardens, the result of centuries of careful cultivation.

When A.E.H. arrived in October 1877 St John's was a medium sized college with about 100 undergraduates. A.E.H. was given rooms off a stair from the Second Quad and quickly made friends with A. W. Pollard another scholarship student. A.E.H. seems to have started in good spirits, writing home to tell Mamma, Lucy Housman, of how he had gone through the Matriculation ceremony, learning to write his name as Alfredus Edvardus Housman. He was amused by the the initiation ceremonies and the rules which said that among other things, he was not allowed to use firearms or trundle a hoop in College.

He was a quiet, confident student and in those early days seemed to

The Gateway to St John's

take a keen interest in people and politics and what was going on in the college and the University. He was, however, from the start critical of the standard of classical scholarship which prevailed. The direction of classics at Oxford stemmed from Professor Benjamin Jowett, Master of Balliol, who felt that the purpose of the University was to turn out people broadly educated, equipped for the professions and the Civil Service. Here he took the very opposite view from the young Housman who had already committed himself to detailed scholarship for its own sake. A.E.H. only went to one lecture by Jowett and came away disgusted by his apparent disregard for the niceties of scholarship.

At first A.E.H. applied himself to the required work. He was taught mainly by tutors in his own college but also went to Magdalen for special lessons from a Fellow named T. H. Warren. In his second term he was entered for the very prestigious Hertford Scholarship for Latin. He did not win it but came creditably in the first six.

At some point he started to follow his own interests and began work on the text of Propertius, a Roman elegiac poet, one of whose themes was unhappy love. He showed markedly little interest in reading the works of classical authors for philosophical content. He preferred textual analysis.

He showed that he had poetical ambitions by entering for the Newdigate Prize which had been won previously by, among others, Matthew

Arnold and Oscar Wilde. The subject for the year was Iona; he came third.

Here in Oxford as at home he walked for relaxation, long walks through the countryside, once as far as Bicester, often with A. W. Pollard.

At the end of the second year A.E.H. had little difficulty in achieving a First in Moderations, as the examinations are called.

In the third year Pollard moved to the other quad and A.E.H. became increasingly friendly with Moses Jackson, a fellow student who was reading Natural Sciences. Moses was a very different type of person from A.E.H.; he was a rower and an athlete, lively and, though intelligent, not particularly intellectual.

In the second half of the degree course philosophy was a more important element in the curriculum but A.E.H. continued to pursue his own interests. Perhaps he felt that he could read enough just before the examinations to satisfy the authorities.

So came the fourth and last year. A.E.H. had to move out of college, into lodgings and he, together with Pollard and Jackson, took five rooms in a picturesque old house nearly opposite the college in St Giles. It was taken for granted that he would do well in his final examinations, Greats. He continued to live a quiet student life, appearing to read a great deal and now not taking much interest in the general life of the college. After dinner in Hall, Pollard, Jackson and A.E.H. would go back to their rooms and Jackson and A.E.H. would sit up late together. They were forming a close friendship. Jackson seemed to

get by without putting in long hours of study. Perhaps in science the syllabus was less demanding. A.E.H. continued to work on the text of Propertius, probably to the exclusion of books which he should have been reading. A few days before his final examinations bad news arrived from home. A.E.H.'s father had had a stroke and was very ill. At the examinations A.E.H. made almost no attempt to answer some of the papers. In August the results were announced. He had failed to qualify for a degree.

Young is the blood that yonder
  Strides out the dusty mile,
And breasts the hillside highway
  And whistles loud the while,
  And vaults the stile.

Yet flesh, now too, has thorn-pricks,
  And shoulders carry care,
Even as in other seasons,
  When I and not my heir
  Was young and there.

On miry meads in winter
  The football sprang and fell;
May struck the land with wickets:
  For all the eye could tell,
  The world went well.

Yet well, God knows, it went not,
  God knows, it went awry;
For me, one flowery Maytime,
  It went so ill that I
  Designed to die.
                              From MP XXXIV

His friends and tutors were shocked and behind the scenes the examiners pondered over the situation only to decide that failure was inescapable.

Canterbury Quad

Later A.E.H. agreed they had no choice.

A.E.H. never explained. His friends and family speculated as to the reason for this extraordinary failure and biographers sift the evidence. To some it is enough that A.E.H. arrogantly refused to read prescribed books that did not interest him. To others the disturbing news from home was the cause. And to others still it was the diversion of spending time with Jackson that should have been spent studying. Perhaps all these played their part but something else, which surely was crucial, was the emotional upheaval of finding that his friendship with and admiration for Moses Jackson had gone far beyond a simple friendship. It was a love that he could not speak of nor come to terms with, and which he could share with no one - least of all Moses.

We do know that A.E.H. was stricken when he heard the results of Greats and returned home to Perry Hall a sad figure. However arrogant he was about his scholarship it is hard to believe that he wilfully risked failure and put a huge barrier in the way of of his classical ambitions. He responded with grim resolution. It was open to him to take further examinations to achieve a pass degree and he studied at home through the summer to take up this option, as well as studying for the Civil Service examination. And he continued his work on Propertius.

A.E.H. returned to St John's for the Michaelmas term. He took the examinations the following June. He failed in one subject, political economy, but was considered worthy of a degree. He left St John's expressing a wish to remain a member and to keep his name on the books. He did not take up the degree until he was appointed to the professorship of Latin at **University College London.**

A.E.H. never blamed Oxford for his failure. He later said that Oxford had little effect on him but that there he met his greatest friend. He always

St Giles in the 1880s

spoke of himself as an Oxford man, especially when he was at Cambridge. He always followed the boat race and supported Oxford.

Eventually St John's recognised his worth. He was offered and accepted an honorary fellowship in 1911. He rejected honorary degrees offered in 1928 and 1934.

* *Oxford is easily accessible from London and other parts of England by rail. By road it is just off the M40.*

* *The Tourist Information Centre is at Old School, Gloucester Green, Oxford OX1 2DA. Tel. 01865 726871. There are many publications about the University, the colleges and the museums.*

* *St John's College is open to visitors most days in the year from 1.00 pm to 5.00 pm. Visitors may wander through the quadrangles but there is no access to* buildings other than the Chapel and Dining Hall. The Front Quad with the Chapel and Dining Hall and the Canterbury Quad are virtually as A.E.H. saw them. A.E.H.'s rooms were off a staircase from the Canterbury Quad but there is no record of which one.

The Library is only accessible to bone fide students on application to The Librarian, St John's College . It contains various materials by and about A.E.H. Much of this is in two collections; one was purchased from A. S. F. Gow in 1934, the other was presented by John Sparrow in 1984.

Visitors at opening times can see the lawns and gardens. The lawns were used for archery and elementary tennis and A.E.H. used to play the latter with Pollard.

St John's also owns the pencil portrait of A.E.H. by Francis Dodd illustrated earlier.

The telephone number of the College is 01865 277300.

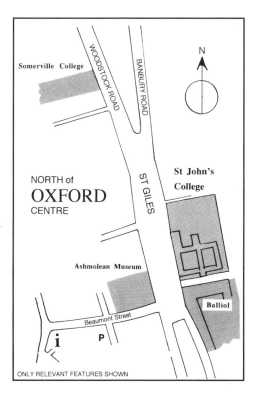

Somerville College

WOODSTOCK ROAD

BANBURY ROAD

N

ST GILES

St John's College

NORTH of

OXFORD

CENTRE

Ashmolean Museum

Balliol

Beaumont Street

i   P

ONLY RELEVANT FEATURES SHOWN

Other Oxfordshire Connections - Souldern and Epwell

Where A.E.H. liked to stay with Percy Withers

Dr Percy Withers was a kindly man who worked hard to make friendships a success. He was appointed Vice-president of the National Medical Services Board in Cambridge during the First World War. One afternoon soon after Withers had arrived in **Cambridge,** A.E.H. knocked at his door with an introduction from his publisher, Grant Richards. From that time a friendship developed, fostered with kindly persistence by Withers. They met every few weeks while Withers was in Cambridge and, when he left in 1920, Withers began a frequent correspondence. He bought an eighteenth-century house in Oxfordshire, Souldern Court, in the village of Souldern, north of Bicester. This part of Oxfordshire is the valley of the Cherwell, fairly flat, but has, good Midland scenery. It is on the edge of the Cotswolds with pretty villages.

Souldern happened to be very close to the route A.E.H. took when being driven from Cambridge to **Woodchester** on his annual visits to the Wise family and in June 1921 he asked if he could break his journey and call in for lunch with the Withers. The occasion must have satisfied A.E.H.; the next year he called again and stayed for three days. After that a summer visit became an annual event in A.E.H.'s calendar and Withers and his family did everything they could to please

Souldern Court

him. This meant giving him good meals and leaving him alone to read in the library or the garden and not intruding upon him with conversation. Withers habitually went on two long walks a day, four to six miles each, and A.E.H. accompanied him, much of the time in silence. Withers reminiscences are recorded in a book, *A Buried Life*, which is full of revealing anecdotes and enigmas. A.E.H., he said, showed little awareness of nature or landscape on these walks and did not stop to admire the flowers in the hedgerow bottoms. In the garden of Souldern Court, however, with its stone walls, summerhouse and terraces, its ancient yews and its walnut trees, he did spend time in the morning admiring the flowers, burying his face in blossom; it was the scent that seemed to give him special delight. Because A.E.H. and Withers shared an enthusiasm for church architecture a regular feature of the visits was an all-day motor tour of Midland churches .

In 1934 Withers moved about twenty miles to Epwell Mill, a house of grey-brown stone with attractive gardens, set in a hollow under the smooth curves of hillier land. A.E.H. was to come here only once, when in spite of failing health, he climbed the nearby hill and commented on the pleasure that was given by the Oxfordshire views.

* Souldern is just off the B4100 (formerly A41) between Banbury (8 miles) and Bicester (7 miles). Approaching by motorway, the M40, it is 3 miles from Junction 10 in the Banbury direction.

* Souldern Court, a private house, is right in the centre of the village at the crossroads, overlooking the village pond. The artist Paul Nash was another of Withers' friends. He did several paintings of the pond and considered them among his best. Some of them are now in Somerville College , Oxford, library together with Withers' letters from poet and artist friends, including A.E.H.

* Epwell is 7 miles from Banbury, just to the right of the B4035. Epwell Mill is between Epwell and Shutford.

Epwell Mill is a private house, down a drive and cannot be seen from the road. The garden is open several times a year under the National Gardens Scheme - for details see its yellow book - and for access at other times groups can apply in writing. The gardens are delightfully landscaped with lawns, pools and borders, beautifully planted.

Here also, Paul Nash used to come and paint.

Epwell Mill

London

The late Nineteenth Century

A.E.H. went to live in London in 1882. He was to spend the next twenty-nine years there.

A.E.H. must have had very mixed feelings about going to London in November 1882. He was going to the Metropolis, the largest city in the World, the heart of the greatest empire the World had ever known, a seat of learning. It was a city, which had expanded rapidly through the century, and was still expanding. The population of London was increasing both with the high birthrate and as more and more people were drawn in from the country. Housing developments spread and engulfed surrounding villages in the great mass of Outer London. The main railway and underground networks were in place but ever more people worked in central London and the horse-drawn traffic steadily increased. There were huge numbers of horse-drawn buses and Hansom cabs so that the main streets were heavily congested and very noisy as iron-shod hooves and iron-rimmed wheels bit into stone-surfaced roads. Horse droppings were churned to muddy slurry in wet weather, and in dry, to choking dust. Smoke poured from every chimney. In November the fogs would be at their worst, impenetrably laden with soot. At night the streets were dimly lit by gas lights. And there were the poor, Dickensian poor, in slums that smelt of open drains.

Fleet Street - about 1890

But it was also the London of grand Georgian developments, Buckingham Palace, Regent Street, the British Museum. A.E.H. had been to London, as a boy of nearly sixteen, for a few days with his stepmother's sister, Mary Theophania Housman, and his earliest surviving letter, written to his stepmother, was sent home from there. He tells how he saw many of the sights of central London. He walked about the City, where, though he did not know it, he would be working a few years later.

He went to the **British Museum** which was to become so important to his life in London and he spent most of the time there in the Greek and Roman galleries. 'I like' he said 'the view from Westminster Bridge, and Trafalgar Square best of all the places I have seen, and I am afraid you will be horrified to hear that I like St Paul's better than Westminster Abbey; The Quadrant (Upper Regent Street), Regent Street, and Pall Mall are the finest streets; but I think of all I have seen, what has most impressed me is - the Guards. This may be barbarian, but it is true.' He had played at soldiers as a child at Perry Hall and his continued fascination with soldiering later came out in a number of poems.

London, when he arrived to work at the **Patent Office**, would have attractions as a base for future scholarship. He would escape the stifling problems at home and would be able to continue his friendship with Moses Jackson, but he would miss the countryside as is brought out in a number of poems.

Give me a land of boughs in leaf,
  A land of trees that stand;
Where trees are fallen, there is grief;
  I love no leafless land.

Alas, the country whence I fare,
  It is where I would stay;
And where I would not, it is there
  That I shall be for aye.

And one remembers and forgets,
  But 'tis not found again,
Not though they hale in
    crimsoned nets
  The sunset from the main.

MP VIII

The Patent Office

A.E.H. was a clerk at the Patent Office from November 1882 until early 1892.

When A.E.H. failed Greats at St John's College, Oxford, and at the same time financial problems were pressing at home, a decision as to what to do was required. The Civil Service was a natural avenue for a person of his station. We can also suppose that an added attraction of the Civil service was that Moses Jackson had chosen this career. With his good science degree Moses had entered the Patent Office, at a salary intended to lure scientists away from academic careers, and he soon became a Patent Examiner.

In the summer of 1882 A.E.H. returned to Oxford to take examinations to qualify for a Pass degree and he also took and passed the Civil Service examinations. Through the autumn at **Perry Hall**, to the concern of his stepmother he waited for jobs to come up, refusing to apply for one 'in Ireland. In November he was offered a job in the Patent Office, off Chancery Lane, London, a Higher Division Clerkship in the Trades Mark Registry. It was probably more than chance that Moses was already established there. The post was not as lowly as we would think from the modern usage of the word clerk; the grade was intended to provide candidates for high administrative and policy-making posts. It was not highly paid but then it was not highly demanding, requiring only six hours commitment each day. It would give a living and allow time for his real interests.

The Patent Office building where A.E.H. worked was in Southampton Buildings which lies just off the northern end of Chancery Lane. It was a Georgian building wherein the Patent Office had been given temporary accommodation in 1852. Ten years before Housman started there it had been condemned as absurdly deficient and soon after he left it was described as being 'the dingiest, dirtiest and most ill-suited building in London' and pulled down. It had a presentable facade but behind was a rabbit-warren of corridors leading to depressing rooms and, worse still for A.E.H., the Trades Mark Registry where he worked was in one of a huddle of ill-assorted buildings at the rear and opening onto a narrow cul-de-sac, Quality Court, which emerged a little farther down Chancery Lane. All this was in the busy, crowded, smoky City. No wonder a few of A.E.H.'s poems were to cry out for the country and unsurprisingly he chose to live well away from the City in the suburbs.

In the office he was one of a number of clerks scrutinising applications and comparing them with marks already registered. In his early years the volume of work was very high. The Trades Mark Act of 1875 had created the need for registration and it was the Victorian period when there was a great growth in trade and invention. The work was such that meticulous attention to detail was required and, although we can be sure that A.E.H. would be wishing he could devote the time to classics, it

The Patent Office of 1852
Where A.E.H. worked - later pulled down

was a type of work for which he was temperamentally suited and he endured it for ten years.

It must however have been a period of some considerable trial. At first it would seem as though it were for ever. The salary, starting at £100 a year, was very modest and permitted only a frugal style of living. Everything in A.E.H.'s later life showed a man who was contemptuous of those who did not match the very high standards he expected in anything he did. He must have been a critical and difficult subordinate. At one time he was picked to become Private Secretary to the Head of the Office. It did not last long. He was too outspoken when he did not agree with his boss and he resented having his carefully worded drafts amended. He also probably resented having to adopt the Civil Service style and conventions. It is clear that he never contemplated a career in the Civil Service; it provided a living, but his real interest in life was his classical studies.

There is nothing to see of the buildings in which A.E.H. worked. The Victorian building which stands at 25 Southampton Buildings, off Chancery Lane, and which has 'Patent Office' carved in its stonework was built between 1898 and 1901 on the same site as the previous Georgian building. It now houses the British Library, Science Reference and Information Service.

Similarly the old buildings which housed the Trades Marks Section of the Patent Office facing Quality Court were rebuilt in 1903.

The one thing you can do, given that the street pattern is unchanged, is to get a feel of how claustrophobic these courts must have seemed to Housman coming from the country.

Life and Lodgings in Bayswater, 1882-1886

Arriving in London in December 1882, A.E.H quickly picked up the friendship he had made at **St John's, Oxford** with Moses Jackson. His first lodgings were in 15 North Place, Bayswater, where he lived alone for a few weeks. By early 1883 he was established in 82 Talbot Road, Bayswater, with Moses and his

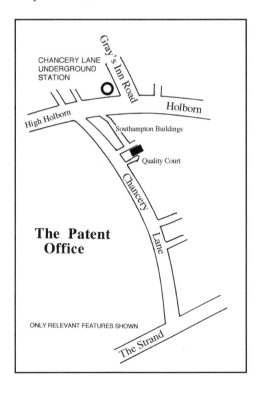

brother, Adalbert, who was studying classics at **University College London**.

Bayswater was a development that grew rapidly from 1840 across an area north-west of Hyde Park where springs had provided the greater part of the water supply for the city. By the 1880s it was a smart district of streets, terraces and squares, joining North Kensington and Shepherds Bush. It was on the Circle Line of the Underground and, as well as having easy access to Hyde Park, the countryside was still not far away.

The three young men apparently lived happily together for three years. A.E.H. appears to have been absorbed in their company largely to the exclusion of family and other friends. His brother, Laurence, and sister, Clemence, had come to study in London and, though A.E.H. saw something of them, he did not invite them to meet Moses and Adalbert and he even made A. W. Pollard, who had shared lodgings with Jackson and himself in Oxford, seem unwelcome at this time.

He began to pursue classical studies at the **British Museum** in the evenings, though probably not with great intensity. He did not achieve publication of any papers in those years. It was a time of settling in to London life.

From the wash the laundress sends
My collars home with ravelled
    ends:
I must fit, now these are frayed,
My neck with new ones London-
    made.

Bayswater housing - Talbot Road
The actual house that A.E.H. lodged in with the Jackson brothers is gone

Homespun collars, homespun
    hearts,
Wear to rags in foreign parts.
Mine at least's as good as done,
And I must get a London one.
                    MP XXIX

Then in the autumn of 1885 A.E.H. disappeared from his lodgings for a week. It is generally inferred that there was a some crisis in the relationship with Moses Jackson. It may have been that A.E.H. revealed the full extent of his feelings for Moses, having concealed them since they were together at **St John's, Oxford**. The revelation would probably be a considerable embarrassment for

Moses who simply wanted friendship as college chums. During the week of absence Moses became concerned and exchanged worried letters with A.E.H.'s father. When A.E.H. reappeared, he made arrangements to move to other lodgings in 39 Northumberland Place, Bayswater, where he lived alone for a number of weeks. Continuation of the happy camaraderie of student days was over.

> By bridges that Thames runs under,
>   In London, the town built ill,
> 'Tis sure small matter for wonder
>   If sorrow is with one still.

> And if as a lad grows older
>   The troubles he bears are more,
> He carries his griefs on a shoulder
>   That handselled them long before.

From ASL L

Talbot Road is about a third of a mile north-west of Bayswater underground station. No. 82 where A.E.H. lodged with the Jacksons has been pulled down but much of the housing of the time remains to give a feel of the area.

39 Northumberland Road is still there and bears a blue plaque commemorating A.E.H.'s short stay.

39 Northumberland Road
Bayswater
A.E.H.'s brief refuge is now marked
with a blue plaque

Moses Jackson

Adalbert Jackson

Byron Cottage, Highgate & Yarborough Villas, Pinner

Where A.E.H. lived from 1885. In Byron Cottage most of 'A Shropshire Lad' was written.

In 1886 A.E.H. left Bayswater. He had found Byron Cottage, in Highgate and was installed in lodgings with Mrs Hunter. It must have suited him, he stayed until 1905 and then, when Mrs Hunter moved to Yarborough Villas, Pinner, he moved with her.

Byron Cottage is quite large to be called a cottage. It remains unaltered, a red-brick, double-fronted, tile-roofed, Georgian building with a ground floor, a first floor, where A.E.H. had his room close to the bathroom - important to a very private man - and an attic floor with dormer windows. Its white windows and central, period, front door give it a charming appearance. It was called Byron, not after the poet, but after an earlier inhabitant who was, in 1757, a Governor of Highgate School.

Byron Cottage is in North Road, close to Highgate village and Highgate Hill, which are on a high ridge north of London. Highgate is the place where legend says that Dick Whittington heard the bells of London and turned back to make his fortune. In the eighteen eighties it was a quiet sleepy village with a remarkable number of public houses. Surrounded by farms, woods and common land, it was seen as a healthy refuge from the smoke of the city and, though housing developments were already spreading up from Kentish Town, this is probably why A.E.H. chose to live there. It is a short walk to Highgate Wood and Hampstead Heath.

When A.E.H. arrived at Byron Cottage he had resolved to concentrate his mind on studies, which he had kept going, but not pursued vigorously during the years with the Jacksons in Bayswater.

How clear, how lovely bright,
How beautiful to sight
  Those beams of morning play;
How heaven laughs out with glee
Where, like a bird set free,
Up from the eastern sea
  Soars the delightful day.

Byron Cottage, Highgate

Today I shall be strong,
No more shall yield to wrong,
  Shall squander life no more;
Days lost, I know not how,
I shall retrieve them now;
Now I shall keep the vow
  I never kept before.

From MP XVI

So now, more regularly, he was at the British Museum after work at the Patent Office submitting himself to the discipline of concentrated work.

A very short time after separating from the Jacksons he was writing to Macmillan proposing that they should publish his edition of Propertius. They did not accept this and A.E.H. settled down to work on other aspects of Greek and Latin. By 1892 he had twenty-five papers published in classical journals. These publica-

tions were the key to a successful academic appointment at **University College London**, as is covered later in this chapter.

While at Byron Cottage A.E.H.'s recreation was walking. He had walked around Bayswater with the Jackson brothers and he went walking with friends from the Patent Office, John Maycock and M. H. Eyre. With the latter two friends he spent whole Sundays in Surrey ending with meals at such inns as the White Horse at Shere and the Angel at Guildford.

* *Both these hostelries are there to be enjoyed as A.E.H. did.*

Writing a Shropshire Lad

A.E.H. also took many solitary walks and it was when walking that poems came to him. He later said that he wrote most of A Shropshire Lad in a few months in 1895 while suffering from 'a relaxed sore throat' In fact he was writing from the late 1880s but from 1890 until 1896 when 'A Shropshire Lad' was published there was certainly a period of intense creativity culminating in the early months of 1885 when about a third of the poems in A Shropshire Lad were written.

During time leading up to this prolific creative period he was subject to a number of emotional stresses. A more distant relationship with Moses Jackson had not damped A.E.H.'s feelings and it was a sad parting when Moses left to take up a teaching appointment in India in 1887.

Having drunk a pint of beer at luncheon - beer is a sedative to the brain, and the afternoons are the least intellectual portion of my life - I would go out for a walk for two or three hours. As I went along, thinking of nothing in particular only looking ,at things around me and following the progress of the seasons, there would flow into my mind, with sudden and unaccountable emotion, sometimes a line or two of verse, sometimes a whole stanza at once, accompanied, not preceded, by a vague notion of the poem which they were destined to form part of. Then there would usually be a lull of an hour or so, then perhaps the spring would bubble up again. I say bubble up, because, so far as I could make out, the source of the suggestions thus proffered to the brain was an abyss which I have already had occasion to mention, the pit of the stomach. When I got home I wrote them down, leaving gaps, and hoping that further inspiration might be forthcoming another day. Sometimes it was, if I took my walks in a receptive and expectant frame of mind; but sometimes the poem had to be taken in hand and completed by the brain, which was apt to be a matter of trouble and anxiety, involving trial and disappointment, and sometimes ending in failure. I happen to remember distinctly the genesis of the piece which stands last in my first volume. Two of the stanzas, I do not say which, came into my head, just as they are printed, while I was crossing the corner of Hampstead Heath between the Spaniard's Inn and the footpath to Temple Fortune. A third stanza came with a little coaxing after tea. One more was needed, but it did not come: I had to turn to and compose it myself, and that was a laborious business. I wrote it thirteen times, and it was more than a twelvemonth before I got it right.

This extract from the Leslie Stephen lecture, *The Name and Nature of Poetry*, by A. E. H. 1933, illustrates how he wrote poems

He would not stay for me; and who
   can wonder?
   He would not stay for me to
      stand and gaze.
I shook his hand and tore my heart
   in sunder
   And went with half my life about
   my ways.

AP VII

And though Moses returned on
leave there was another wrench when
he married in 1887 and only told
A.E.H. afterwards.

Then Adalbert Jackson, with whom
A.E.H. had continued a strong friendship, died suddenly in 1892, just after
A.E.H. had become Professor of Latin
at University College.

Oh, many a month before I learn
   Will find me starting still
And listening, as the days return,
   For him that never will.

From MP XLII

And, while A.E.H. was detached
from Bromsgrove and the family, he
must have been aware of the
problems of his father's health and
finances. In 1894 Edward Housman
died and A.E.H. returned to mourn at
Catshill.

The last ten years had been a stressful time of terminating relationships
and it is not surprising that, when his
health was below par, emotions
should come welling up.

As the poems came to him with
increasing intensity in the early
months of 1895 A.E.H. formulated the
intention to publish and by March
1896 *A Shropshire Lad* was on sale.

And on to Yarborough Villas.

A.E.H. had taken up his professorship at **University College London** in
1892 and he continued to live a quiet
life at Byron College. The years went
by and in 1905 Mrs Hunter decided to
move to 1 Yarborough Villas, Pinner
and A.E.H. moved with her. It gave
him farther to travel to university but
he was comfortable with Mrs. Hunter
and she respected his privacy. When
in 1911 he moved out to go to **Cambridge** she generously said she was
pleased because he did not see
enough people while living with her.

* *Byron Cottage, 17 North Road,
Highgate is a private house, easily identified with its blue plaque. It is about half a
mile from Highgate tube station and a
few hundred yards from Highgate village.
North Road is now a busy one-way road
with traffic lanes but it is easy to imagine
a quieter era.*

* *Even now there is still a village feeling
about Highgate and A.E.H. would recognise many of its buildings. Hampstead
Heath and Highgate Wood are still to be
enjoyed. And you can have a pint of beer
at the Spaniard's Inn as he did.*

* *The Pinner address was 1 Yarborough
Villas, Woodridings, Pinner. Yarborough
Villas were a new development when Mrs
Hunter moved there, on the estate of a
large house with a lake. They in their
turn have been replaced by newer
suburban housing. One pair of the old
villas remains.*

One of the Yarborough Villas

structed between 1823 and 1857 to the designs of Robert Smirke, and fine classical designs they are too. It contained then a very good collection of artifacts from Greece, Rome, Egypt and Asia. The famous Round Reading Room, where Karl Marx, Mahatma Gandhi and George Bernard Shaw in their time worked, was there too, having been added in 1857. Its grand dome is wider than that of St. Peter's in Rome.

When A.E.H. at 15 visited the British Museum with Mary Housman he was already fascinated by classical Greece and Rome and was very knowledgeable too. He had been told by his step-mother to look out for the Towneley Venus but he wrote home to say he preferred the Mercury from the Farnese Palace in Rome. He must in later years have frequently visited the Galleries of the Museum and he wrote in *A Shropshire Lad* one of his heart felt cries:

> Loitering with a vacant eye
> Along the Grecian gallery,
> And brooding on my heavy ill,
> I met a statue standing still,
> Still in marble stone stood he,
> And steadfastly he looked at me.
> 'Well met,' I thought the look
>   would say,
> 'We both were fashioned far away;
> We neither knew, when we were
>   young,
> These Londoners we live among.'

From ASL LI

The British Museum and Library

A.E.H. admired the Farnese Mercury in the Museum when he was 15 and later, between 1883 and 1892 studied in the Library to establish his reputation as a scholar.

In A.E.H.'s youth the British Museum and Library was already a proud institution. It was founded in 1753 and the main buildings were con-

In Housman's time up to and including the 1890s both the Towneley Venus and the Farnese Mercury were in the Graeco-Roman

Room so, although it is Roman, he could still have had the Farnese Mercury in mind when he wrote the above poem.

After he went to work at the **Patent Office**, A.E.H. used the Library to continue classical studies. He began to study intensively from 1888 when

he had moved to **Byron Cottage**. After finishing his day at the Patent Office he would frequently spend the evening in the Library before returning to his lodgings. Here his early classical papers were written.

* The British Museum is in Great Russell Street, WC1. Tel 0171 636 1555. It is open 10.00 am-5.00 pm Monday-Saturday, 2.30 pm-6.00 pm Sunday, except public holidays. Tottenham Court Road is the nearest Underground station.

The Graeco- Roman Salon
The British Museum 1875

* *The galleries have been changed. The old Graeco-Roman Room now forms part of the approach to the public restaurant. The Farnese Mercury can still be seen in the gallery housing Roman sculpture, one of the Wolfson Galleries in the basement under the Duveen gallery.*

Also in the Wolfson Galleries, Room 85, (The Towneley Room) includes the Towneley Venus

* *The Library of the British Museum became the British Library in 1978. It is moving out into new premises about 1997. Meanwhile the Round Reading Room is accessible to the public from the British Museum through hourly guided tours. Otherwise it is only accessible by enquiry before a visit to the Reader Admissions Office, Great Russell Street, London WC1B 3DG. Tel. 0171 323 7677.*

After the British Library has moved it is planned that the Round Reading Room will retain a library/reference function and be incorporated into enhanced facilities at the Museum.

The British Museum

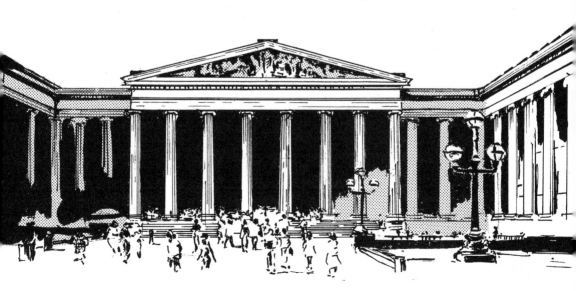

University College London

In 1892 at the age of 33 A.E.H. made the amazing transition from Patent Office clerk to Professor of Latin at UCL. He was there until 1911.

University College London was founded in 1826 and first opened to students in 1828. It was the original University of London and is still the largest of the institutions that make up the University. It has a liberal tradition; it was the first university in Britain to be open to all religions, races, classes and political persuasions and the first to open its doors to women. Its entrance is off Gower Street in Bloomsbury. Behind the quadrangle lies the main facade of the imposing, classical-styled building, with a large portico and columns, designed by William Wilkins, who also designed the National Gallery.

A.E.H. applied for the professorship in April 1892. His years of working in the evenings at the British Museum had led to the publication of papers in the leading classical journals, the *Classical Review* and the *Journal of Philology*, and they had attracted the attention and admiration of some of the most eminent classical scholars of the day. No less than fifteen of them added testimonials to his letter of application. He was accepted.

Although to get a professorship from the basis of a pass degree and no academic experience was no mean achievement, we need to be aware that at UCL the Latin department was quite small. Arts in general and classics in particular had been in the doldrums at UCL but within a period of a few years three significant appointments were made. First in 1889 W. P. Ker was made Professor of English. In 1892 Housman was appointed to the Latin chair and then in 1894 Arthur Platt became the Professor of Greek. The combination of these three led to a great strengthening of the intellectual standard of the Arts and to a flourishing social life in the College.

In October 1892 A.E.H. gave an introductory lecture on the aims of learning which was a great success and was printed by the college and widely distributed; quite an achievement for some one new to academic life.

A.E.H. must have quickly adapted to university teaching. He was required to carry out a heavy programme of lecturing by professorial standards, for he had no assistants - he was the Latin department - and the standard of the students was not high. This meant that much of the teaching was fairly basic, probably not higher than A level in today's terms.

His style was reserved, aloof and unapproachable but in spite of that he soon earned the respect of his students and of fellow academics. His arrogant contempt for those of lesser scholarship, apparent at Oxford and in papers that he had published since must have made him a formidable figure to students, but many found that he was capable of being kindly, if only in an austere fashion.

The early years at UCL were busy with teaching and stressful in his private life and he was in the state of fervour in which he was writing *A Shropshire Lad* in his spare time at Byron Cottage. Nevertheless he began to build on his stock of published classical material. He began his major work of textual criticism on the Latin astronomer/astrologer poet, Manilius. He chose Manilius, not for the intrinsic merit of what Manilius had to say – there are differing opinions on this – but for the interest and challenge of elucidating the texts. It was something A.E.H. was uniquely equipped to do having an interest in astronomy in addition to his other accomplishments. The first volume of Manilius was published in 1903 by Grant Richards at A.E.H.'s own expense. He was not however confining himself to

UCL in the early twentieth century

Manilius; he worked on other Latin and sometimes Greek authors and in 1905 an edition of Juvenal was published. But Manilius was his major preoccupation. It was to take until 1930 to complete all four volumes.

Under the three professors the Literary Society at UCL flourished and over the years Housman presented a series of papers on poets including Arnold, Burns, Swinburne and Tennyson. In addition he became a popular speaker in the college, in debates and more informally as an after-dinner speaker where his astringent wit was much appreciated. He was persuaded from time to time to contribute facetious verses to the student magazine. One of these was *The Amphisbæn*a or, *The Limits* of

Human Knowledge which was about the mythical two headed serpent. It began:

If you should happen to descry
An Amphisbæna drawing nigh,
You may remain upon the spot,
But probably had better not.
The prudent its approach avoid
And do not stop to be annoyed,
For all who see it are perplexed
And wonder what will happen next.
Both ends, unfortunately, are
So singularly similar.

A.E.H. was also treasurer of the Professors' Dining Club where he displayed a great knowledge of food and drink.

It was natural that at some stage he would move on; his scholarship merited a more prestigious appointment and he wanted one which would give him more time to carry out his textual researches. He saw the right opportunity in 1910 when the Kennedy Professor of Latin at **Cambridge** died. A.E.H. applied, was accepted and took up the appointment in the spring of 1911.

* UCL is situated on the east side of the north end of Gower Street. The Front Lodge, the Quadrangle and the facade of its main buildings are very similar to

University College London today

what they were in the 1880s, though the side of the Quadrangle facing Gower Street which was open has been almost filled in with additional buildings, so that today the space of the Quadrangle comes as a surprise as you enter.

* *It is permitted to walk around some of the main buildings, and a guide is issued from the Friends Room. This is just behind the Lodge on the right .*

* *In the Quadrangle are several cherry trees given by the Japanese Branch of the Housman Society in 1976 in memory of A.E.H..*

Under the dome of the portico is the Main Library . On either side on the ground floor are the Cloisters. Off the North Cloister is the senior common room which is dedicated the Housman Room. In the North Cloister is a small exhibition with displays featuring famous people who have studied or taught at UCL, including A.E.H.. There is a copy of his letter of application.

* *There are Housman records in the Manuscripts and Rare Books Room of the Bloomsbury Science Library (approached from Torrington Place.) The collection comprises books about Housman and various archives and autographs including A.E.H.'s letters to his stepmother and to Mrs. Platt. Access is granted to bone fide students on production of adequate identification or a suitable letter of introduction. Enquiries should be made to the Librarian, University College London, Gower Street, London, WC1E 6BT. Tel 0171 3807796.*

A.E.H. in 1896

Changing London

During those years from 1882 to 1911 when A.E.H. was at University College considerable changes were taking place in London. It had continued to grow and was still very congested. First bicycles and then motor cars joined the horse-drawn traffic. By the end of this period there were nearly as many motor vehicles as horse-drawn vehicles.

From the beginning of the period electric street lighting began to replace gas, and shopwindows began to be lit. In 1890 electricity was first introduced to power the Underground trains. The city was however still a sooty and dirty place.

Where a 'A Shropshire Lad' was published

A Shropshire Lad was first published in 1896 by Kegan Paul, Trench, Trubner & Co. Ltd in an edition of 500 copies. It was published at A.E.H.'s own expense.

A.E.H. had gathered the poems together under the proposed title of *Poems by Terence Hearsay*. He asked his friend A. W. Pollard from Oxford days to read them and Pollard suggested the title, *A Shropshire Lad*. Pollard also suggested Kegan Paul as publisher.

Kegan Paul operated from Paternoster House, a good Victorian brick building, that the firm had built for itself close to the Garrick Theatre in Charing Cross Road, opposite Bear Street. The first edition of 500 copies came out in March of 1896. It was a small slim book in a pale blue board cover measuring, 172 x 110mm It had some good reviews but was slow to gather success.

The first edition of *A Shropshire Lad* caught the attention of a young man, Grant Richards, who was starting his own business as a publisher. He wrote to A.E.H. who came to see him at his offices in Henrietta Street, then an important artery of Covent Garden fruit and vegetable market. As a result of that meeting by mutual agreement A.E.H. extricated himself from the connection with Kegan Paul and *A Shropshire Lad's* second edition came out in September 1898 under the imprint of Grant Richards.

Richards recorded his impressions of his first meeting with A.E.H. in the book he wrote, *Housman 1897-1936.*

'I fell, and I fall back on the word 'precise'. For my visitor was precise, agreeably precise, but precise. Precise, as I have said, in speech, bearing, clothes. And economical - economical of words. And sombre? Yes, I have used that word and I will stick to it. He was rather sombre. And I feel that he remained a little sombre to the end. But we know that to his friends he was not altogether or greatly sombre. I am however concerned at this moment with the man of 1898. There was nothing eccentric on that day in his appearance, his behaviour, his clothing. A dark and unpretentious suit - I think a short black coat and waistcoat, both cut rather high at the neck, and striped trousers - elastic-sided boots - elastic-sided boots were in no way eccentric in those days - a bowler hat, an umbrella, an air of preferring to pass unnoticed through the streets. I had seen scores of such men - as far as clothing went - at Oxford walking down 'the High' and around Mesopotania.'

The second edition was in a green buckram cover, 132 x 85mm, even smaller than the first.

From then on *A Shropshire Lad* was never out of print. Grant Richards continued to publish it. A.E.H. stayed with him even when he got into financial difficulties and had to sell his business and start up again in 1904, this time in tiny rooms in Carlton Street on the corner of St Alban's Place.

Over the years Richards became a personal friend of A.E.H. They dined together frequently and went together on a number of continental holidays.

Their friendship even survived another of Grant Richards bankruptcies, but this time *A Shropshire Lad* stayed with the new owners of the business which became Richards Press.

*   *Paternoster House, the birthplace of ASL, is still there in Charing Cross Road. It is divided on the ground floor into shop units but the upper floors still show that it had style and symmetry.*

*   *9 Henrietta Street where A.E.H. often talked to Grant Richards about ASL is once more a publishers office. Grant Richards left it for offices in Leicester Square in 1901. These have been demolished.*

What was Paternoster House

Cambridge

Arrival in Cambridge

A.E.H. came to Cambridge as Kennedy Professor of Latin and Fellow of Trinity College in 1911. He was to stay there until his death in 1936.

A.E.H. was 52 when he took up his professorship. He was not a total stranger to Cambridge. When he was still at the **Patent Office** the quality of his published classical papers had been noticed and he was invited to join the prestigious Cambridge Philological Society. He had travelled to Cambridge frequently by train from London for its meetings.

Today he would still recognise much of the heart of Cambridge. From the Middle Ages it had grown as the most important East Anglian trading centre on the small but navigable River Cam. The road from London ran into the High Street and this converged at the top of the town with the road from the south-east; between them was the market place. The High Street was later segmented and renamed as Trumpington Street, King's Parade and Trinity Street. The road from the south-east became Sidney Street and St. Andrew's Street.

Cambridge was already a thriving town when scholastic institutions began to develop in the early thirteenth century and from then on the university grew along with the com-

College rooftops
A corner of Trinity Great Court
in the foreground

mercial aspects of the town.

A major grouping of colleges was developed on recovered wetland between the High Street and the river during the fourteenth, fifteenth and sixteenth century. Gradually over seven centuries, the college buildings were erected, gardens were set out, bridges were built, the banks of the Cam were landscaped and trees were planted and so we have The Backs, surely one of England's finest sights; its trees and green swards setting off mediaeval stonework and the elegant pinnacles of King's College chapel reaching up from the line of colleges.

It was all there when A.E.H. came. The town had a population of about 40,000. It was expanding fast, spreading out across the fields to Grantchester, Trumpington and Cherry Hinton but this did not disturb the seclusion of the college courts and gardens.

Trinity College

Where A.E.H. found sanctuary and scholarship for all his years in Cambridge.

The University at Cambridge is the central body which provides coordinating administration, lectures, the University and specialist libraries, sets examinations and awards degrees. The Kennedy Professorship was a University appointment. The Colleges are separate and largely self-governing, providing accommodation, libraries, tuition and seclusion to study. Trinity College was quick to offer A.E.H. a Fellowship.

Trinity is the largest of the Cambridge colleges. It lies between Trinity Street and the Backs, flanked by St John's (which was A.E.H.'s grandfather's, The Rev Thomas Housman's, College) and Trinity Hall and Gonville & Caius. To say that Trinity College was founded by King Henry VIII in 1546 does not do full justice to its lineage for even then it was created by amalgamating two existing colleges, the King's Hall and Michaelhouse, both of which originated in the early fourteenth century and among the colleges were only predated by Peterhouse.

The Great Gate, which is the principal entrance to Trinity, is in Trinity Street. It was built as the entrance to the King's Hall between 1490 and 1535.

The Great Gate leads into the magnificence of the Great Court which was inspired by the vision of Thomas Nevile who became Master of Trinity in 1593. To put this vision into effect he had the Clock Tower, which was also built as an entrance to the old King's Hall , moved into line with the Chapel which was built between 1555 and 1567. He had ranges of buildings, which had been erected since the founding of Trinity, and which intruded on his design, pulled down. He included the old hall of Michaelhouse in the square and completed it with new buildings. He rounded off the landscaping with the fountain in early seventeenth-century style. The Great Court is the largest and most impressive court in Cambridge

When that was complete, Nevile moved on to begin the development of a further court, Nevile's Court,

The Great Gate, Trinity College
About 1920

which is approached via the steps which rise to the Hall on the west side of the Great Court. Nevile's Court was completed in the 1690s by the erection of the Wren Library which is one of Sir Christopher Wren's most perfect works.

The Years at Trinity

1911 was a year of transition for A.E.H. He was appointed to the Kennedy professorship in the spring and he was still nominally professor at **University College London** for the summer. During this period he took lodgings at 32 Panton Street and still spent time at **Yarborough Villas** finding the quietness he wanted to prepare his lectures for the autumn.

His first duty at Cambridge was to give an inaugural lecture which he did in May. As well as covering his subject, textual criticism, he took the opportunity of stating his debt to B. H. Kennedy, in whose honour the professorship had been created. The book, *Sabrinae Corolla*, which had set A.E.H. on his classical career, after it had been given to him as a prize at **Bromsgrove School,** had been edited by that same Kennedy, while head of Shrewsbury School.

A.E.H. had much to be pleased about with his appointment. It was very prestigious. He would have less requirement for lecturing than at University College London. He would be expected to devote himself to the advancement of his subject, which was exactly what he wanted to do. The one thing he thought he would miss was his solitude that had been a feature of the years with Mrs Hunter at Byron Cottage.

This problem was solved to some extent when Trinity College found

him rooms in Whewell's (pronounced Hewell's) Court. This is really a group of three courts. The stone buildings in neo-gothic style were completed in 1868. The main entrance is opposite the Great Gate in Trinity Street and the buildings run through to Sidney Street. A.E.H. was able to choose a suite of rooms at the rear, on the second floor, off K staircase, close to the Sidney Street entrance. This secluded, cheerless, eyrie was from then on his home for all but a few weeks of his life.

He had a sitting room a small bedroom and a study. When working he sat at a table piled with books, in a straight-backed chair, a pair of dumb-bells by his side with which he exer-cised from time to time to ward off drowsiness. Beside a fireplace were photographs of Moses and Adalbert Jackson. Another picture was of the

St John's, Oxford, Eight in which Moses Jackson rowed. The bedroom was narrow, cold and austere.

From here in Whewell's Court he settled into a pattern of life. Like clockwork he appeared just in time for lectures and for meals at High Table in Hall. In the afternoons he took long walks, slipping out into Sidney Street. He would often go out of Cambridge, past the Botanic Gardens and into the flat countryside with its pollard willow-lined water-ways beneath the wide East Anglian

The Great Court, Trinity College - the largest in Cambridge - looking north

On the left is the Hall and on the right the Great Gate. In the centre is the Clock Tower flanked, on its left by the building where A.E.H. had rooms during his last year, and on its right by the Chapel, behind the fountain

skies. As motor buses appeared in the twenties, he ventured further for new starting places for his walks and to discover different villages.

A.E.H.'s lectures, of which he gave two a week during term time, were attended by staff as much as students. They were highly respected by those who appreciated the ideals of scholarship which he projected. They were demanding. One erstwhile student, the Rt Hon Enoch Powell remembered:

'He read his lectures word for word, standing ramrod-straight in the smallest of the lecture-rooms - for Housman was caviare to the general - never apparently looking to see what impression, if any, he was producing upon his hearers. At the beginning of a term a number used to come out of curiosity to see what the famous poet looked like; but after the first lecture or two only a hard core would remain faithful. His face as he read was expressionless, and the effect, especially with the overhanging moustache and bald cranium, was of a voice proceeding from the mouth of one of those masks which the actors wore on the Greek tragic stage. The only movement of the body likely to be observed was a quick prefatory wielding of the window pole to exclude the hated draught from above his rostrum. The lecture being read -

Whewell's Court

always precisely fifty minutes in length - he donned his mortar-board and stalked impassively back to his fastness above the Jesus Lane entrance to the repellent pile of Whewell's Court.'

During his years at Cambridge A.E.H. was able to give time to his work on the text of Manilius. The second volume was published in 1912, the third in 1916 and the fourth in 1920. There was then a ten year interval before the final volume was published in 1930. This edition of Manilius was A.E.H.'s major work, his monument he called it, but it was not his sole scholastic preoccupation. He produced editions of Lucan and Juvenal and throughout his professorship he published classical papers regularly on a range of Latin, and sometimes Greek, authors.

Meanwhile writing poetry was a low key activity for most of his time at Cambridge . The fervour that was with him in the run up to 1896 when *A Shropshire Lad* was published had abated. He wrote on average less than two poems a year and he ignored the pleas that came from his publisher, Grant Richards, and his friend Percy Withers, to write more. When the Muse came, it came. What is more, he rarely discussed poetry at Cambridge. His academic colleagues soon found that he wished to keep this aspect of his life to himself. There was however one period in 1921 and early 1922 when something of the fervour which produced *A Shropshire Lad* returned. It has been attributed to the terminal illness of Moses Jackson now far away

We'll to the woods no more;
The laurels all are cut,
The bowers are bare of bay
That once the Muses wore;
The year draws in the day
And soon will evening shut:
The laurels all are cut,
We'll to the woods no more.
Oh we'll no more, no more
To the leavy woods away,
To the high wild woods of laurel
And the bowers of bay no more.

Autograph of introductory poem to 'Last Poems'

in Canada. A.E.H. wrote enough new poems, together with his output of the last twenty years, to make up his second volume, *Last Poems*. This small book was published by the Richards Press in the autumn of 1922 and by the end of the year 21,000 had been printed to meet the demand from a long-waiting public.

In spite of A.E.H.'s reticence and desire for solitude there was a strong social aspect to his life in Cambridge. He sat for dinner at High Table in Trinity with illustrious company. In his early years the table would include such powerful intellects as G. H. Hardy, mathematician, J. G. Frazer of Golden Bough fame, J. J. Thomson, the physicist who discovered the electron and became Master of Trinity,

G. M. Trevelyan the historian, and Bertrand Russell, G. E. Moore and Ludwig Wittgenstein, philosophers. There were also many occasions when he was invited out to dinner. To some he was known as a difficult dining companion. He could be reticent in the extreme and cutting in his remarks but also, in the right mood, witty and amusing.

A.E.H. took a strong interest in some aspects of College life. His knowledge of wines earned him a place on the Wine Committee and he regularly made entries in the Kitchen Suggestion Book. Examples:

'As venison is now about half the price of mutton it is our duty to have it sometimes in the interests of economy.' - 23 September 1916.

'When there is no R in the month it may be necessary to have egg-sauce with cod, but the evil day should not be anticipated as it was yesterday. (This does not apply to the salt cod on Ash Wednesdays and Good Fridays for which egg-sauce is quite proper).' - 19 April 1928

He was very fond of the College gardens. He was delighted by the drifts of crocuses on the Backs in the spring. He recorded the dates of coming into leaf and flowering of plants and trees. He took a keen interest in the planting of the cherry trees along the Avenue on the Backs in 1926. He spoke of the expected loveliness when they matured and flowered although he could not hope to see it.

As the years went by, A.E.H. developed a pattern of life in which the summer recess usually included a trip abroad. Often this took the form of three or four weeks in France where he would hire a car and be driven round, exploring the architecture of churches and enjoying good food and wine. He also travelled to Rome and Venice. In 1920 he became one of the first paying passengers to fly over the channel, which was regarded as very risky, and from then on chose to use this method of transport whenever possible. Grant Richards, his publisher would sometimes accompany him on his continental trips.

Also part of the summer pattern were visits to the Wise family in **Woodchester**, to Percy Withers in **Souldern**, to his brother, Basil, and his wife in **Tardebigge**, and to his sister, Katherine Symons, in **Bath.**

A.E.H. was 70 in 1929. He had used up his three score years and ten. He considered himself fit but his doctor said his heart was not as strong as it should be. He was about to complete his Manilius and, when he went to France that summer, he travelled by train and ship, taking care of his life. After the edition was finished, he carried on doing all the things he enjoyed doing, but he said that though life was tolerable he would be happy to go.

In 1933 he was persuaded to give the Leslie Stephen Lecture and chose as his subject 'The Name and Nature of Poetry'. The preparation of the lecture was a considerable torment to him but, when it was delivered in May, it was greeted with great

Petty Cury about 1920

acclaim. It was during this lecture that he expressed the view that the function of poetry was not to transmit thought but emotion and he said that, 'Experience has taught me, when I am shaving of a morning, to keep watch over my thoughts, because, if a line of poetry strays into my memory, my skin bristles so that the razor ceases to act.'

Shortly after the lecture A.E.H. had to spend a time in the Evelyn Nursing Home in Cambridge. His heart had deteriorated. From then on it was a struggle to keep up the pattern of his life, though he did so with stoical determination. Between spells in the Evelyn he continued both lecturing and his habit of taking walks. He climbed his stairs two at a time, he wrote, 'in the hope of dropping dead at the top'. In 1935 he paid his last visits to the Withers, now at **Epwell**, and to **Tardebigge** for a family gathering and a last visit to the **Clock House**. He took his last holiday in France.

In October 1935 the College arranged for him to be transferred to ground floor rooms in B Great Court so that he would have no stairs to climb. He spent Christmas in the Evelyn. He struggled on giving lectures to within a few days of his death, sometimes being taken by taxi from the Evelyn.

He died on 30 April 1936. There was a funeral service in the Chapel at Trinity - a chapel that, as an atheist, he had not attended. His brother, Laurence, said he did believe in 'a Supreme Being' but not a Personal Deity. The hymn that he had written for the occasion was sung.

FOR MY FUNERAL

O thou that from thy mansion,
  Through time and place to roam,
Dost send abroad thy children,
  And then dost call them home,

That men and tribes and nations
  And all thy hand hath made
May shelter them from sunshine
  In thine eternal shade:

We now to peace and darkness
  And earth and thee restore
Thy creature that thou madest
  And wilt cast forth no more.

MP XLVII

The coffin was covered by a mass of white cherry blossom from the College Avenue. A.E.H. was cremated and later his ashes were buried by the surviving members of his family at **Ludlow** parish church.

Cambridge

* *Cambridge is 50 miles from London. It is easily accessible by train with a frequent service from King's Cross and Liverpool Street. By road the main route is the M11*

* *The Tourist Information Centre is in Wheeler Street. Tel. 01223 322640.*
There is a wealth of information, books. pamphlets etc. about the town, the University and the colleges.

Trinity College

* *Trinity College opens The Great Court and the Chapel and sometimes Nevile's Court to the public, from, as this book goes to press, 10.00 am to 6.00 pm daily. There are charges in summer for those who are not Members of the University or residents of Cambridge. The College is completely closed during a period in May / June when examinations are taking place. These arrangements are subject to change.*

* *The Chapel is where A.E.H.'s memorial service was held. There is a brass plaque immediately to the left of the entrance door to the Ante-Chapel. The inscription is in Latin; translated it reads:*

'This inscription commemorates Alfred Edward Housman, who was for twenty-five years Kennedy Professor of Latin and a Fellow of the College. Following in Bentley's footsteps he corrected the transmitted text of the Latin poets with so keen an intelligence and so ample a stock of learning, and chastised the sloth of editors so sharply and wittily, that he takes his place as the virtual second founder of textual studies. He was also a poet whose slim volumes of verse assured him of a secure place in the British Helicon. He died on 30th April 1936 at the age of seventy-six.'

* *When the Great Court is open visitors can usually see Nevile's Court from the passage beside the Hall even when walking*

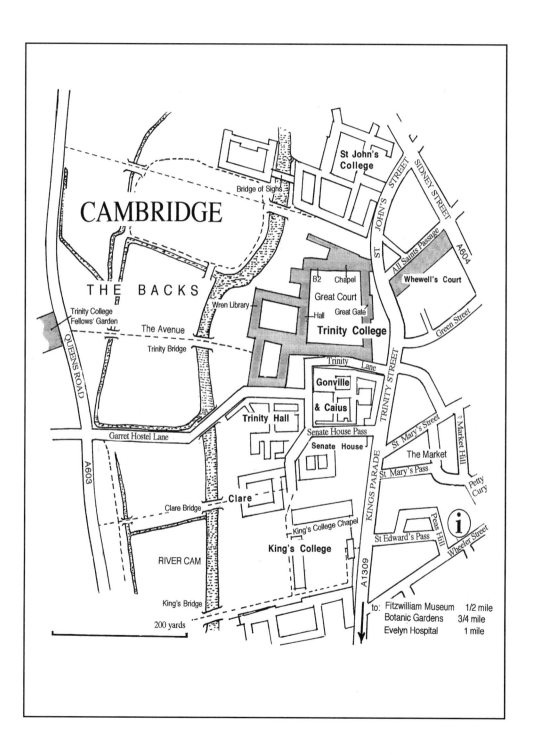

CAMBRIDGE

THE BACKS

St John's College

Bridge of Sighs

Trinity College Fellows' Garden

Wren Library

B2 Chapel
Great Court
Hall Great Gate
Trinity College

Whewell's Court

ST JOHN'S STREET

SIDNEY STREET

All Saints Passage

A604

Green Street

The Avenue

Trinity Bridge

QUEENS ROAD

Trinity Lane

Gonville & Caius

Trinity Hall

Garret Hostel Lane

A603

Senate House Pass

Senate House

TRINITY STREET

St Mary's Street

St Mary's Pass

The Market

Market Hill

Petty Cury

KINGS PARADE

Clare

Clare Bridge

King's College Chapel

King's College

St Edward's Pass

Peas Hill

Wheeler Street

ℹ

RIVER CAM

King's Bridge

200 yards

A1309

to: Fitzwilliam Museum 1/2 mile
Botanic Gardens 3/4 mile
Evelyn Hospital 1 mile

through it is not permitted The Hall is where A.E.H. would dine at High Table.

* *The Wren Library has separate opening arrangements. It is open to the public from 12.00 noon to 2.00 pm Mondays to Fridays, and also from 10.30 am.to 12.30 pm on Saturdays during Full Term. When the rest of the College is not open it can be approached via the Avenue on the Backs.*

It possesses the autograph manuscript of 'A Shropshire Lad', in which each poem is neatly written on separate sheets of lined foolscap. It is often on display in the glass cabinets which are there for the benefit of visitors.

The Wren Library also has a number of letters written by A.E.H. including a number to A. S. F. Gow. Gow was a younger Fellow who achieved friendship with A.E.H. and was his first biographer.

The material in the Library is accessible to bona fide scholars by appointment, on prior application to the Librarian, and with an appropriate letter of introduction.

* *Trinity College also owns drawings of A.E.H. by William Rothenstein and Henry Lamb.*

* *Whewell's Court where A.E.H. had his rooms is not open to the public. His rooms were on the second floor overlooking Sidney Street.*

* *The Avenue across the Backs from Trinity Bridge is flanked on each side by a row of lime trees and a row of cherry trees. The cherries which A.E.H. saw planted in 1929, and anticipated their fine display, died of a fungal disease in the 1980s. They have been replaced.*

* *There is a Japanese cherry tree donated by the Japanese Branch of the Housman Society in 1976 in the Fellows' Garden on the other side of Queens Road.*

The Garden is open to the public once a year in the Spring under the National Gardens Scheme (The Yellow Book).

* *For further information about Trinity College contact the Junior Bursar, Trinity College, Cambridge, CB2 1TQ. Tel. 01223 338400.*

Also in Cambridge

* *The house, 32 Panton Street, where A.E.H. lodged on first arriving in Cambridge still exists. Panton Street runs north from Bateman Street which is the road along the north side of the Botanic Gardens.*

* *A.E.H. gave the autograph manuscript of 'Last Poems' to the Fitzwilliam Museum. It is accessible to bone fide scholars by prior application to the Keeper of Manuscripts , Fitzwilliam Museum, Trumpington Street, Cambridge. Tel 01223 332900.*

* *The Evelyn Nursing Home, where A.E.H. died, still exists, much expanded, as a hospital. It is on the east side of Trumpington Road just south of the Botanic Gardens.*

Woodchester & Bath

The Woodchester Haven

A.E.H.'s mother came from Wood-chester. He visited it as a child and found friendship and comfort with the Wise family all his life.

Stroud in Gloucestershire is set in the southern Cotswolds. This is country of swift, flowing streams which have carved steep-sided valleys out of the limestone plateau. The hillsides are rounded and often wooded. The fields are thickly tree-lined and the valleys are sheltered and green. The buildings are of a variety of Cotswold stone which weathers to pleasant shades of yellow and grey. Stroud itself, a substantial town, has grown up where five valleys converge. It is a town of steep slopes and different levels, with houses creeping up the hillsides, tier upon tier.

The valley running south is the Nailsworth Valley. Through it flows the Nailsworth Stream , which used to power a series of woollen mills; wool being the original staple industry of the Cotswolds. Beside the stream runs the road to Bath and at one time a railway ran through too. Strung out along the western slopes of this valley are North and South Woodchester and behind them rises Selsley Hill.

The largest house in North Woodchester is Woodchester House. It is secluded, set in trees and shrubberies and approached by a curving drive It was built about 1740 of dressed stone, and has a classical Georgian facade. The broad symmetrical frontage has a pedimented, central front door,

flanked by two windows on each side. There are three storeys. Behind the small windows on the top floor were the servants' rooms. The house is deep as well as broad, and a special feature is the impressive hall which goes right through to the back of the house. Altogether it is a substantial residence.

Here William Housman (brother to A.E.H's grandfather), came to live in 1827 with his wife, Mary, and a growing family, which in Victorian fashion continued to grow. William had made a good marriage, for Mary was a Vernon of **Hanbury Hall** near **Bromsgrove**. He had practised as a solicitor in Bromsgrove before moving to Woodchester.

Mary mothered ten children including Henry and Lucy Agnes. Henry is worth a mention; in his youth he formed a museum in Wood-chester House and wrote a book about it, *The Story of our Museum*. Henry became a cleric, a calling which ran in the Housman family. Lucy however is of greater relevance, for not only did she eventually become stepmother to A.E.H., but her influence began even before that.

Her friend as a child was Sarah Jane Williams, the daughter of the rector of Woodchester, and when Edward Housman, father of A.E.H., came from Bromsgrove to visit his relatives in Woodchester, she introduced him to Sarah Jane, and that led in due course to their marriage.

William and Mary Housman lived in Woodchester House for about twenty-five years, though with some interruption, moving out and moving back. Their apparently happy occupation ended when William went one day on a routine business trip to London and was not seen again. It is said that he absconded with an actress and went to America. Mary Housman stayed in Woodchester for a time but eventually moved, probably returning to Bromsgrove. In 1851 the Wise family moved into Woodchester House.

The three families of Woodchester, the Housmans, the Williams and the Wises, which are important in the background and life of A.E.H. have now been introduced. The Rev John Williams was rector of the church in Woodchester from about 1833 until 1857 when he died. He had formerly been curate-in-charge at Stroud. He was a well-educated man, a classical scholar who wrote both poetry and hymns and was descended on his mother's side from the Drakes of Devon of which Francis Drake was a member. His church was a small Norman building, which had been built in the ruins of a 4th century Roman villa in North Woodchester, since famous for its mosaic pavement that still lies buried there. He lived with his wife and family in the Rectory. He died in 1857 and his daughter, Sarah Jane, and Edward Housman were married in his church in 1858, having delayed their plans because of his illness and death.

Sarah Jane's roots were in Woodchester. She still had many friends there and she kept up her connections, even though she lived in Bromsgrove. Particular friends were the Wises.

Woodchester House

Edward Wise was a businessman in the wool trade. Though the best years of this trade were over, he was obviously prospering when he moved into Woodchester House after William Housman's family had left and later in 1868 he acquired Woodchester Mill, the biggest in the valley. He and his wife, Elizabeth, had three children, Edward Tuppen, Edith ('Edie'), and Wilhelmina ('Minnie'). Mrs Wise was godmother to Alfred and it was with the Wises that Sarah Jane would stay when she visited Woodchester.

Just after the marriage of Sarah Jane and Edward Housman, a new church was being built in Woodchester to replace that of which John Williams had been rector. The latter was too small and had been allowed to fall into a bad state of repair. The new church was formally consecrated in 1863. Edward Wise, who was a churchwarden and had given the land for the church to be built on, provided a substantial dinner for three hundred people in a marquee to celebrate the consecration. Edward and Sarah Jane Housman were there and Edward responded to the toasts. He said his father and grandfather were clergymen and he hoped his son would be a bishop - it was not to be!

All did not go well in relations between the Housmans and the elders of the new church. Sarah Jane together with her mother had a memorial window dedicated to her father put in the chancel. This led to great controversy in the parish, for the design and wording were considered 'Romist'. Dr Williams is referred to as a 'priest' in the inscription and a minister of a foreign church is depicted in the window. Sarah Jane forcibly rejected the accusations in an open letter which was printed as a pamphlet and distributed in the village. The controversy did not lessen Sarah Jane's love of Woodchester and she imparted that love to Alfred. She must have talked of the place with affection to him in the nursery at Bromsgrove and, when he was seven in 1866, she took him to stay with the Wise family. An impressionable boy, he quickly adopted Woodchester as a special place and the Wises as special people. He was to return many times right until the end of his life.

The Wise children were older than Alfred. When he was seven Edward Tuppen would be fifteen, Edith would be twelve and Minnie would be ten. They had a German governess, Sophie Becker who was about twenty-two. They all liked Alfred and involved him in their games, rambles and family life. So began his lifelong deep affection for the Wise family, Sophie Becker and Woodchester.

Alfred's second recorded visit to Woodchester was when he was almost twelve. This was when his father sent him away during the last days of his mother's illness and the news of her death at **Perry Hall** actually came on his twelfth birthday. At this time Mrs Wise lived up to her promises as godmother and the assurances that she had given to Alfred's mother when she knew she was dying. With the Wises he was given comfort and sympathy and he became a frequent visitor to Woodchester during school holidays. He became at least as much part of their family as his own. Perhaps they meant even more to him because at Woodchester he could escape the constant reminders of his late mother and the problems of his father's finance and alcoholism.

He was particularly friendly with Edith Wise, so much so that his brothers and sisters joked at his expense saying that he was in love with her. His affection for Sophie Becker, perhaps transferred from his mother, was even stronger and at the end of her life and close to the end of his life, he was to refer to her with great tenderness as one of the three real friends he had ever had.

When he was away from the Wises he would write to them amusing letters and comic poems, something which he also did in the visitors' book at Woodchester House (now in the library at Indiana University, U.S.A.).

Elegant Edith and modest Minnie
A-walking along by the side of a
    spinney.

Modest Minnie in front proceedeth,
And close behind trots elegant Edith.

When out of the spinney a midge
    arises
And taketh and biteth the two Miss
    Wises.

"Oh something has just come out of
    the spinney
And taken and bitten me, modest
    Minnie."

"Oh elegant Edith, you need not
    squall so,
For something has taken and bitten
    me also."

"Oh modest Minnie, by what are we
    bitten?
A tortoiseshell cat or a tabby kitten?

What animal is it whose venom
    rankles
In both of our modest and elegant
    ankles?

A mouse or a midge that lives in the
    spinney
Or a cow or a crocodile, modest
    Minnie?"

"Oh elegant Edith, it does not matter;
Carbolic will do us more good than
    chatter.

Whatever it is, it's a nasty creature
Whose conduct has no redeeming
    feature.

For of all odd acts it is quite the
    oddest
To bite the elegant and the modest."

Here ends the tale of the two Miss
    Wises,
It might be true if it wasn't lieses.

Visits and letters continued until 1878, A.E.H.'s second year at **St John's, Oxford,** when relations between the Wises and A.E.H.'s father reached a crisis. In 1874, Edward Wise (senior) died at the age of 65. The Wise family found that they were still well enough off to continue living in Woodchester House but not as well off as they had thought. In 1875, Alfred's father's continuing financial problems came to a head. He involved Edward Tuppen, much to his detriment, in machinations over the mortgage on **Perry Hall** and borrowed money from him. The Wises were shocked and worried and eventually took legal action.

Alfred heard about this and felt that he could not continue his visits, although the generous-spirited Wises did not hold him responsible. The financial problem was ultimately resolved by an uncle of Edward Housman who bought Perry Hall and allowed Edward and his family to live there but it was not until nine years later in 1887, when Alfred was employed by the **Patent Office**, that he made contact again with the Wises and took up the friendship with renewed intensity. From then on annual visits became a part of his life. It is easy to imagine that, when London was oppressive and Bromsgrove full of hurtful memories and problems, Woodchester was detached, undemanding and full of happy companionship.

So the years went by. The Wises got poorer. At first they took in paying guests while still keeping up the responsibilities that fall on generous inhabitants of the large house in a village. In 1911 Mrs Wise died and Edward Tuppen moved the family to Oakley House, which although still a substantial house, better matched their diminishing means. As an economy Sophie Becker was asked to leave after more than forty years with the Wises and returned to Germany. A.E.H. corresponded with her but never saw her again. None of the three younger Wises married. Edith died in 1930 and Wilhelmina in 1931. Edward now alone moved to a much smaller house, Elmsleigh, where he

died in 1934 a few months after A.E.H. had paid his last visit.

The Woodchester connection was ended. The news of Sophie Becker's death came a few months later. One by one the people who had been important in A.E.H.'s life were diminishing in number.

* *Stroud is most easily approached by road from the north or west by the M5. It is about 6 miles from junction 13. From London the best route is along the M4 to junction 15 and on the A419 through Cirencester.*

By rail it is directly accessible from London and Birmingham and from other places via Gloucester or Cheltenham.

* *There is a tourist information centre in the Subscription Rooms, George Street, Stroud. Tel. 01453 765768.*

* *Woodchester is one and three quarter miles from the centre of Stroud on the A46. There is first a sign for a right hand turn to North Woodchester (Selsley Road) and then a little further on a sign to South Woodchester (Station Road)*

* *From Stroud Woodchester can be reached by buses en route from Gloucester to Nailsworth.*

* *Let us assume that you have arrived by car and will walk around the village - you can drive but the roads are narrow and it is difficult to park. The following is a circular walk with two fields to cross but otherwise on hard pavement ,which takes you by the most Housman-relevant places. It is about a mile and a half long.*

Probably the best place to park is in Southbank by the church. To get there take the turn to North Woodchester from

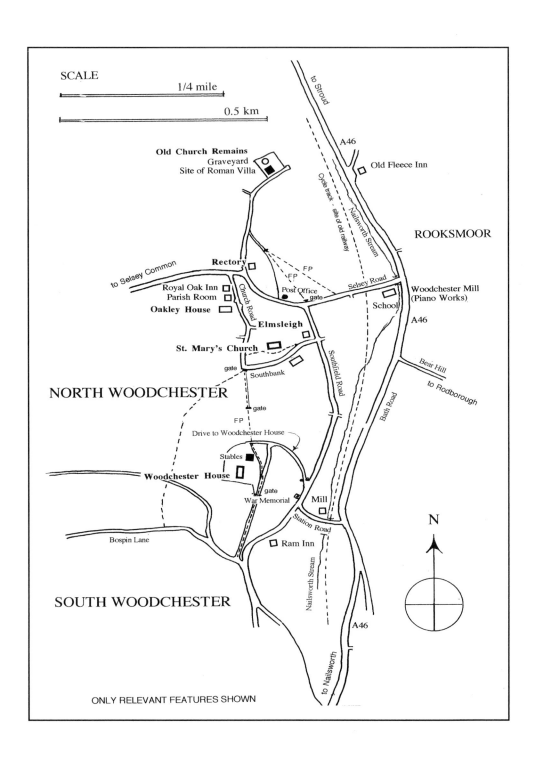

SCALE

1/4 mile

0.5 km

Old Church Remains
Graveyard
Site of Roman Villa

to Stroud

A46

Old Fleece Inn

ROOKSMOOR

Cycle track - site of old railway

Nailsworth Stream

to Selsey Common

Rectory

FP

FP

Post Office

Selsey Road

Woodchester Mill
(Piano Works)

Royal Oak Inn
Parish Room

Oakley House

Church Road

gate

School

A46

Elmsleigh

St. Mary's Church

Southfield Road

Bath Road

Bear Hill

to Rodborough

gate

Southbank

NORTH WOODCHESTER

gate

FP

Drive to Woodchester House

Stables

Woodchester House

gate

War Memorial

Mill

N

Station Road

Nailsworth Stream

Bospin Lane

Ram Inn

SOUTH WOODCHESTER

A46

to Nailsworth

ONLY RELEVANT FEATURES SHOWN

the A46. As you turn the Piano Factory is on the corner . This was the site of the **Woodchester Mill** which Edward Wise owned. It was burnt down in 1989 and has been rebuilt. Take the second turning left into Southfield Road and the first right which leads to Southbank. The school is on the left and the church is on the right.

At the top of Southbank is a gate on the left and a path which leads through to **Woodchester House**, where William Housman and his family lived from 1827 and the Wises from about 1851 and where A E H frequently stayed.

Woodchester House main gate is near where Station Road meets Southfield Road. From there the tarmaced drive curves across fields to a second gate. The path from Southbank indicated above comes out by this gate.

Woodchester House, is still a private house. It is hidden among trees and shrubbery. The stable buildings are just inside the second gate and, if you keep straight on the track past the stone gates,you pass the boundary of the grounds in front of the house. Continuing straight on would lead to South Woodchester but turn back along the curving drive to the first gate to Woodchester House.

(Station Road drops down in fifty yards to the valley bottom where there are the ruins of a woollen mill, a bridge across the Nailsworth Stream and the bed of the old railway, which is now a cycletrack and footpath between Stroud and Nailsworth. Here in the bottom on the right was the railway station where A.E.H. would arrive for his visits.)

Turn left along Southfield Road . In a few hundred yards the road to the church and Southbank branches off on the left, and on the righthand corner as you look towards the church is **Elmsleigh** where Edward Tuppen Wise saw out his last two years.

Continue along Southfield Road to the junction with Selsley Road and you will see the Post Office. Just below the Post Office go through an iron kissing gate and you can walk across the field and over another metalled road to the site of the **Roman villa** and the ruins of the **old church,** where Dr John Williams preached. This is behind a neat dry stone wall and you can climb over with the help of a step-stile.

The old graveyard is there with some interesting stone 'table' tombs . A drive of old yew trees leads to all that remains of the old church , the early Norman chancel arch and part of the north wall. It has an air of history and seclusion.

Amid the tombs there is a flat grassy area about fifteen yards square. Under this lies the Roman pavement. The villa, of which this formed a part, was a 60-room building dating from the 4th century. The pavement depicts Orpheus charming the birds, beasts and fishes with his music. Earlier in this century it used to be uncovered from time to time and in 1926, on one of his visits, A.E.H. was pressed into service to give guided talks about it. It has not been uncovered since 1973.

Leaving the old churchyard, turn right, ascend and walk back up the road to Selsley Road. Here on the left hand is the Rectory. This pleasant building was built in 1915 on the site of the old Rectory where A.E.H.'s mother was brought up.

Turn right and then left into Church Road. On the right is the seventeenth century Royal Oak, an excellent inn. It is possible that A.E.H enjoyed a pint here more than once. It is a good place to break your walk.

Continuing on your right you pass **Oakley House,** where the Wises moved when they were forced to economise .

Onwards and you come back to South-bank with the new **church of St. Mary** the Virgin which was designed by Teulon, a well known Victorian architect, and built between 1859 and 1863. It is of simple stone work with a broach spire, The once controversial window to the memory of the Rev John Williams is on the north side of the chancel.

The church is kept locked except at service times. There are details posted in the porch about access at other times. There is a pamphlet about the church available inside.

This ends the walk around the village.

* There is much lovely country to see and enjoy in the area. Selsley Road leads up onto Selsley Common with its magnificent views of the Severn estuary, where A.E.H.'s walks would take him to 'look to Wales away'

* One of A.E.H.'s friends was William Rothenstein who was a well known figure in the world of art and who became Principal of the Royal College of Art in 1920. From 1912 he owned Iles Farm at Far Oakridge, five and a half miles away from Woodchester on the Golden Valley. When staying in Woodchester A.E.H. would walk over to see him.

* It is worth mentioning, to avoid confusion if nothing else, that Woodchester Mansion , an unfinished Victorian masterpiece of Cotswold stone, set in grounds owned by the National Trust, is in the area . There is limited access. For information contact Woodchester Mansion Trust, 1 The Old Town Hall, Stroud, GL5 1AP. Telephone 01453 750455.

The chancel arch of the
old church

The Housman Sundial at Bath

In a peaceful setting on a hillside above Bath is the cemetery of Smallcombe and here there is a sundial dedicated to the children of Edward and Sarah Jane Housman.

There is no connection between Woodchester and Bath in A.E.H.'s life other than that he visited both and they are grouped together in this book only on the basis that they are not far apart - about twenty-five miles.

Bath was the home for many years of A.E.H.'s sister Katherine (Kate). She married Edward Symons a gifted academic who had studied at University College, Oxford and as a young man and, by coincidence, (though there is no evidence that they knew each other then), was a Fellow of **St John's College** when A.E.H. was an undergraduate. He then chose to become a teacher and during a time as Second Master at **Bromsgrove School** met and married Katherine. After other appointments he ended as the Headmaster of the King Edward's School in Bath. Kathleen was always the member of the family who was the co-ordinator. She kept a correspondence going with her brothers and sisters and they would visit the Symons family in Bath.

In 1901 Herbert the youngest of the family and a soldier was killed in the Boer War. Then in 1905 Robert, a scientist who had never enjoyed good health, died at the age of 45 while visiting his sister. The Symons family

arranged for him to be buried at St Mary's Cemetery, Smallcombe. The remaining brothers and sisters then got together and had the sundial erected in 1908 to the memory of the lost brothers.

The sundial is an octagonal, fluted pillar of Bath stone. Lead plaques were attached to the octagonal base. One facet identifies the sundial as for 'The children of Edward and Sarah Jane Housman'. Two were for Herbert and Robert. This left five for the surviving brothers and sisters and their names were inscribed in due course. Encircling the base are the words 'Our days on the earth are as a shadow and there is none abiding.' It is a memorial stone - Herbert, Basil, Alfred and Laurence are not buried in the cemetery.

* *Bath is south-east of Stroud and Woodchester on the A46.*

* *Smallcombe cemetery is just over a mile south-east of Bath centre. It can be reached from Pulteney Road,via Pulteney Gardens, Horseshoe Road and Horseshoe Walk. To find the sundial, walk from the cemetery gate past the chapel, towards a slope on the right.*

King Edward's School, founded 1552, still exists as an Independent School in new premises. It used to be in the handsome Palladian-style building that is still in Broad Street.

* *From 1899 the Symons family lived in the Headmaster's House at 20 Belmont on Lansdown Road about 400 yards from the school and here A.E.H. often visited them.*

Shropshire's Poet

Housman is Shropshire's poet. *A Shropshire Lad* not only made him famous but it also did a great deal to make Shropshire well known and well loved. So perfectly do some of his lines capture the spirit of Shropshire that there is hardly a book about the county that does not quote a few of his lines. The settings of the poems (rather than the sentiments expressed) create a picture of a pastoral idyll. The picture is convincing even to Shropshire people.

And yet A.E.H. did not come from the county, never lived there and seldom talked about it. Early reviewers of *A Shropshire Lad* commented on this and writers since have gone to much trouble to try to demonstrate either that he got his knowledge from guide books and friends, or alternatively that there are detailed facts in the poems that he could have obtained only with first hand knowledge.

A.E.H. said little to throw light on the enigma. It was difficult for anyone to get him to enlarge on the background to his poetry . There are just two or three letters in which he commented on Shropshire. He said that he took a romantic view of Shropshire because it was his western horizon in his youth. He said that a few of the poems were written before he had been to Shropshire but he knew

Shropshire

Ludlow and **Wenlock**.

In London, when A.E.H. wrote most of *A Shropshire Lad*, he remembered the country of his youth and he remembered the far country on the horizon with particular sentiment. He was, we have seen earlier, going to call the first collection of poems *Poems by Terence Hearsay* but he was advised by his friend Pollard to change the title. He then went over the collection strengthening the Shropshire identity and visited Shropshire to obtain local colour.

Probably the truth is that A.E.H. knew rather more about Shropshire than he declared and that he deliberately kept people guessing. It is not so difficult to reconcile the apparent authenticity of the Shropshire settings with the fact that he never lived there. You do not have to live in a place to have a feeling for it. He lived close to Shropshire. The rural life he knew in Bromsgrove was very similar and most of the trees and flowers he knew so well were common to both counties. It would need only a few visits to add the magic of Shropshire names and places.

Titterstone Clee and Brown Clee from Fockbury.

Housman's Country

If we plot on a map the towns, villages and rivers named in A.E.H.'s poems we can define Housman's Country. From Fockbury, **Bromsgrove**, he looked across undulating land towards the **Clee Hills**. Beyond the Clees to the west the most distant place mentioned is **Knighton** on the Welsh border, forty miles from Fockbury. The most northerly place he writes about is **Shrewsbury**. These three places, Bromsgrove, Knighton and Shrewsbury mark out a triangle of country which includes both the places he wrote about (excepting **Bredon**) and where he lived. Most of it is a particular part of Shropshire between the River Severn and the Teme.

A.E.H. clearly felt he belonged to **Severn shore**. It would be surprising if he had not made some excursions to the west and there was an easy route to Ludlow when he was a youth and a young man. From Kidderminster, only seven miles from Bromsgrove there were several trains a day to Woofferton just south of **Ludlow.** The line ran through **Bewdley** and on through Wyre Forest. It is the route by which, in reverse, the Shropshire Lad left Ludlow for London.

As through the wild green hills of Wyre
The train ran, changing sky and shire,
And far behind, a fading crest,
Low in the forsaken west
Sank the high-reared head of Clee,
From ASL XXXVII

The train ran through **Cleobury Mortimer**, from where he could have walked up **Titterstone Clee**, and on along the Teme Valley. From Woofferton a main line ran to Ludlow. There is no knowing whether A.E.H. did this but it is clear that South Shropshire was accessible. Indeed the whole triangle of country was contained in rail routes with a main line from Ludlow to Shrewsbury and the Severn Valley line running back down from Shrewsbury to Bewdley.

ONLY RELEVANT FEATURES SHOWN

But a Word of Caution

While the country of the poems is identifiable and the poems are broadly accurate, (notwithstanding the poetic licence with **Hughley** steeple), before the reader goes in search of Housman's Country, it is worth giving a giving a word of caution.

Housman did not set out to describe Shropshire. He created a pastoral setting for the dramas and emotions of his poems. His Shrop-

shire is part truth, part imagined. Its people are totally imaginary and the real Shropshire people are probably much happier than the Shropshire Lad and his friends. Nevertheless South Shropshire is a beautiful part of England and a Housman pilgrim who travels the area, accompanied by *Collected Poems*, is not going to be disappointed. The countryside is as beautiful as he or she will expect and there is far more to see than is mentioned in the poems.

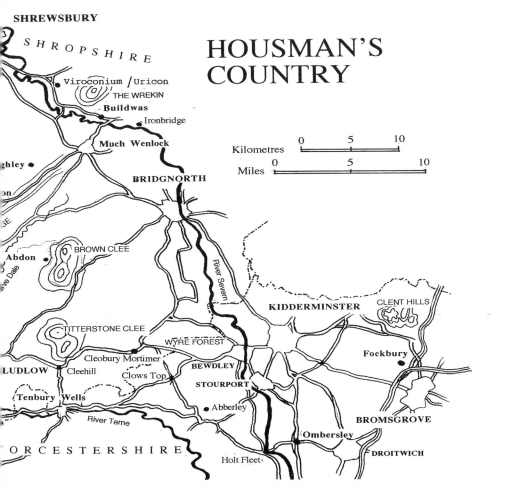

HOUSMAN'S COUNTRY

The Real Shropshire

A.E.H. was romantic about the land on his western horizon. It has been said that wherever he had lived he would have felt that way about the country to the west where the sun set. Maybe, or maybe not, for there is much to be romantic about in this particular western borderland. The **Clee hills**, seen from Fockbury, are sometimes lost in mists, sometimes they are sharp and clear but usually they are a distant blue outline. Through the undulating landscape, that lies before them, the Severn cuts a deep V and forms a barrier which has always made South Shropshire less accessible and, from a Worcestershire perspective, more remotely rural. Beyond the Severn the country grows hillier. Successively there are the Clees, then **Wenlock Edge**, and then Long Mynd and the Stretton Hills and behind them Central Wales.

The character of the country is determined by the geology and the geology is very varied. The Clees are old red sandstone with much older dolerite caps, rich in minerals. Wenlock Edge is limestone from a barrier reef of 450 million years ago. Long Mynd and the Stretton Hills are hard Precambrian rocks, a 1000 million years old.

The history of the area is rich. Between the hills are river valleys that, before man got to work, were thick with oak forest. In prehistoric times it was difficult country where neolithic man created trackways and traded flints. In historic times the Celtic British defended it against the Romans. Their forts are there to see on many hilltops. It was the extreme frontier of the Roman empire. **Viroconium** was the Roman centre of administration for a whole network of forts. After the Romans, the Anglo-Saxons slowly spread across the Severn pushing back the Celts and creating settlements. Offa built his Dyke to designate the limits of his rule. Later the conquering Normans settled this border calling it the Marches and the lords defended it with castles at **Shrewsbury, Bridgnorth, Ludlow and Clun**. It adds up to wave upon wave of successive conflict, settlement and integration. Industrial Britain began along the Severn but then moved to other areas and Shropshire is left rural and relatively thinly populated.

This geology and history combines with other factors to give a landscape which is fascinating. There is the variation of vegetation as the English midlands meet the uplands of Wales, The hilltops, sometimes wooded , sometimes heather or grass, rise over the valleys with their patterns of fields and hedges and standing oaks. There are features such as the rich red soils of Corvedale, the limestone flora of Wenlock, the swift rivers and water meadows, and the scattered hamlets.

The architecture is varied too. Firstly, it is shaped by materials; the legacy of those early oakwoods is a great richness of timbered, black and white, buildings; but with no shortage of different types of stone there are plenty of good stone buildings; and the clays of the valley have ensured a good proportion of brick too. Secondly, the architecture is determined by the long history which gives fine examples of the styles of different periods from the Norman castles and abbey ruins, to churches and to fine houses and cottages of every period.

These are a few hints at the romance of Shropshire. A final touch, which was not missed by A.E.H., is Shropshire's place names. They are deeply imprinted with the history of the area from the simple Celtic 'Clun' and 'Clee' to the magnificent resonance of 'Cleobury Mortimer' with its Norman associations.

* *The rest of this chapter matches the places mentioned in A.E.H.'s poems against the places as they are today. It does not attempt to be a comprehensive guide to Shropshire, or even part of Shropshire.*

* *The main route into Shropshire is via Shrewsbury. Shrewsbury is accessible by Intercity rail services from London. There are also good links to Wales , the Midlands and the north-west. The railway from Kidderminster to Woofferton is long since closed down.*

* *There are no motorways in south Shropshire. The M54 which branches off the M6 leads to Shrewsbury. As it approaches the town it skirts the Wrekin and there are wide green views to the distant line of the Long Mynd and Caer Caradoc.*

The most direct route to Ludlow from the south-east is up the M40 and west along the M42 to Bromsgrove , then the A448 to Kidderminster, and the A456 onwards. This is the subject of the next section of this book.

* *There are a number of Tourist Information Centres covering Housman's Country which have a large range of local literature and offer advice and help find accommodation. The most relevant are:* **Shrewsbury, Bewdley, Bridgnorth, Ironbridge, Ludlow, Church Stretton, Much Wenlock and Knighton.** *Details of these are given later.*

* *For exploration Ordnance Survey maps are invaluable. 137 in the Landranger series covers South Shropshire from Knighton to Clee and north to Much Wenlock. 126 covers Shrewsbury but 127 and 128 are needed to include the Severn valley.*

* *The Housman Society, South Shropshire Trail is a good introduction to Housman and the area (see Ludlow).*

The Gateway to Housman's Country.

Bewdley

The way from the Midlands to Housman's Country beyond the Clees lies through Bewdley; a route travellers have taken to the borderland and central Wales since people inhabited the land. The northern Worcestershire country gently undulates to Severn shore. First there is the substantial town of Kidderminster and then there is Bewdley on the river.

Bewdley is a charming unspoiled ancient town. For centuries it throve on river traffic. The trows, as its sailing barges were called gathered by its quays and teams of men man-hauled them up the fast flowing river or sailed them down to Bristol and the sea. The nineteenth and twentieth century left it unscathed after the the canal from the West Midlands was taken to Stourport. Today the fine bridge built by Telford arches over the Severn and the frontages of its eighteenth century buildings line the river and the main street where the Church of St Anne looks down from its position in the middle of the road.

A mile upstream from Bewdley the Dowles Brook emerges from the Wyre Forest to join the Severn and beside it is the embankment of the railway which used to run through 'Wyre's wild green hills' (ASL XXXVII) and on to Woofferton.

Bewdley, only just outside the Shropshire border, was not named in A.E.H.'s poems but it got very close -

an early draft of ASL XXVIII had Bewdley rather than Buildwas in the line 'When Severn down to Buildwas ran'.

From Bewdley the road climbs out of the Severn valley through the Wyre Forest; a large remnant, thousands of acres, of the oakwood which once clothed the Shropshire valleys.

* *This route west is the A448 from Bromsgrove to Kidderminster and the A456 leaving Bewdley.*

* *Bewdley town is too good to be missed, as you will if you follow the modern bypass . It has an interesting museum which tells the history of the town and the area .*

* *The Tourist Information Centre is beside the carpark just off Load Street. The address is Load Street, Bewdley, Worcs., DY12 2EQ. Tel. 01299 404740*

From Bewdley there are walks up Dowles Brook and on the course of the old railway line into Wyre.

* *Severn Valley Railway runs from Kidderminster to Bridgnorth. There is a stop at Bewdley. This is where the main office is situated: Severn Valley Railway, Bewdley, DY12 1BG., Tel. 01299 403816*

* *Three miles out of Bewdley at Callow Hill the A456 passes the Wyre Forest Visitors Centre. Here you can obtain information about the forest and walks in the area.*

Cleobury Mortimer and Titterstone Clee

Travelling west the country gets more hilly and soon you are approaching Cleobury Mortimer, a small town on the slopes of Titterstone Clee Hill with a delightful name and a church with a crooked tiled wooden spire.

The road to Ludlow actually runs over the high shoulder of Titterstone Clee. There is a cattle grid, the road is then unfenced and crosses the high common land - grassland, studded with tussocks of gorse and grazed by sheep. On a clear day the views are amazing, to the Brecon Beacons, across Herefordshire, to the Malverns and Abberley and over the Severn valley to the Cotswolds.

A.E.H.'s 'high reared head of Clee', (ASL XXXVII) owes its top to the very hard dolerite rock, known locally as Dhustone, which caps the sandstone of the rest of the hill. This stone has long been quarried for road building. The hill also has coal deposits and metals too which were once worked. The scatter of cottages on the sides of the hill is the result of squatting development by miners in past centuries.

The Clees, Titterstone and Brown Clee, are the highest hills in Shropshire. The peak of Titterstone is 1750 feet.

* This route to Ludlow over Titterstone Clee is the A4117 which branches off the A456 four miles out of Bewdley.*

St Laurence's, Ludlow

Ludlow the Capital

Ludlow, the principal town in South Shropshire, and certainly the capital of Housman's Country, is a very visible town set high over the confluence of Corve and Teme. The profile of its red-tiled rooftops is dominated by the castle ruins and its church.

The Buttercross, Ludlow
From a watercolour painting by Louise
Rayner 1829 - 1924

When smoke stood up from Ludlow,
 And mist blew off from Teme,
 And blithe afield to ploughing
 Against the morning beam
 I strode beside my team,
                    From ASL VII

The Normans chose an imposing
and defensible position when the
castle was built. Close to the castle
they laid out the grid pattern of streets
and encouraged the development of
the town under their control - a plan-
tation in the Marches. Packed closely
round the castle, it is one of the most
attractive towns in England. In mediaeval times its buildings were mostly
half-timbered and there are still some

very beautiful examples, the most
famous being the Feathers Hotel,
which has very elaborate carved timbering. Ludlow prospered in
Georgian times as a regional centre of
fashion for the gentry. Some excellent
town houses were built and in this
era many good timbered houses were
given Georgian facades. Fortunately
industry and growth passed Ludlow
by in the nineteenth and twentieth
centuries and its beauty is unspoiled.
It survived as a market town which is
how A.E.H. portrayed it.

Or, come you home on Monday
 When Ludlow market hums
                    From ASL III

He was right. The cattle market
was held on Monday on a site near
the railway station and people came
into the town to sell farm produce.

Ludlow would hum.

The annual fair was an important event in Ludlow's calendar (as it was in A.E.H.'s hometown Bromsgrove) .

> The lads in their hundreds to Ludlow
> come in for the fair,
> There's men from the barn and the
> forge and the mill and the
> fold,
> The lads for the girls and the lads for
> the liquor are there,
> And there with the rest are the lads
> that will never be old.
>
> There's chaps from the town and the
> field and the till and the cart,
> And many to count are the
> stalwart, and many the brave,
> And many the handsome of face and
> the handsome of heart,
> And few that will carry their looks
> or their truth to the grave.
> From ASL XXIII

A.E.H. knew the date of Ludlow fair. It is still held on the first of May in the main streets of the town as it always was.

> The orchards half the way
> From home to Ludlow fair
> Flowered on the first of May
> In Mays when I was there;
> From LP XXXIV

Ludlow has a very imposing parish church, St. Laurence's. Housman was brought up in the shadow of **St John's, Bromsgrove**, and was always extremely interested in church architecture. It is not surprising that St Laurence's features in the poems.

The Recruit

> Leave your home behind, lad,
> And reach your friends your
> hand,
> And go, and luck go with you
> While Ludlow tower shall stand.
>
> Oh, come you home of Sunday
> When Ludlow streets are still
> And Ludlow bells are calling
> To farm and lane and mill,
>
> Or come you home of Monday
> When Ludlow market hums
> And Ludlow chimes are playing
> 'The conquering hero comes',
>
> Come you home a hero,
> Or come not home at all,
> The lads you leave will mind you
> Till Ludlow tower shall fall.
> From ASL III

The chimes really do play 'the conquering hero comes'. The 135 foot tower is a symbol of fifteenth century wealth though much of the church is a great deal older. The overall effect of the architecture is perpendicular but there are many traces of the earlier construction from the twelfth century onwards.

When A.E.H. died the family felt that his ashes should come to Ludlow to lie in his imagined 'Land of lost content'. They were buried under the north wall of St Laurence's mingled with soil and mould gathered from under the trees of Perry Hall and the Clock House, Fockbury.

The inscription on the stone is taken from *Parta Quies*, MP XLVIII, which A.E.H. wrote for his mother.

> Good-night; ensured release,
> Imperishable peace,
> Have these for yours.

* *Ludlow is the obvious base for exploring Housman country. Its Tourist Information Centre is in Castle Street. Tel. 01584 875053.*

* **The Ludlow Branch of the Housman Society publishes a pamphlet which describes a motor trail covering the places of the poems in South Shropshire - Clee, Wenlock, Clun and Knighton. It is available from the Tourist Information Centre or the Secretary , The Housman Society (Ludlow Branch), 37 Lower Broad Street, Ludlow, SY 8 1PH .**

* *The buildings of central Ludlow are mostly the ones which A.E.H. saw though no doubt the town is cleaner and brighter today. The cattle market is still held on Mondays but on a different site, Ox Pasture beyond Ludford Bridge, a mile to the south. There is a street market every day of the week in the town.*

* *St Laurence's publishes a very comprehensive guide to the history and architecture of the church.*

* *Ludlow Festival of the arts takes place during a fortnight in June /July -a good time to visit the town.*

Around Clun -A Western Brookland

The Clun Villages

> Clunton and Clunbury,
>   Clungunford and Clun,
> Are the quietest places
>   Under the sun.

Many people think A.E.H. composed this introduction to ASL L. In fact it is a traditional local rhyme and some say the authentic version was originally 'drunkenest under the sun'. Whichever came first, 'quietest' is certainly appropriate. These villages are in a lightly-populated area very close to the Welsh border. The name Clun has the same origin as the Welsh 'Llan' which means a settlement- the Celts clung on to the area for a long time. West of Clun is the remote Clun Forest, now carrying coniferous plantations. Beyond it is the great central Welsh massif.

ASL L continues.

> In valleys of springs of rivers,
>   By Ony and Teme and Clun,
> The country for easy livers,
>   The quietest under the sun.

This too creates its true picture. The country is hilly and rivers run alder-lined through valleys, 'sleepy with the flow of streams'.

Clun owes its existence to its Norman castle, which is a ruin. It is a large village but it was probably too isolated to prosper as did Ludlow. It has a medieval bridge, a museum with bronze age tools and a church with squat stone Norman tower.

Knighton

Also in ASL L the Shropshire lad remembers his youth as a Knighton lad before he goes to London. (It is no good looking for a consistent story of the origins and adventures of the Shropshire lad for the poems do not link together.)

Knighton, a few miles from Clun, is in Wales, in what was Radnorshire , now incorporated into Powys. It is as much a border town as a border town can be. The modern boundary with England runs along the Teme and Offa's Dyke, the old Saxon boundary, runs through Knighton too.

* *The most direct route to Clun from Ludlow is to go on the A49 to Craven Arms, along the valley of the Onny, as it ripples to meet the Teme, and turn left on the B4368. Clunton, Clunbury and Clungenford are all this side of Clun in a network of smaller roads.*

* *From Ludlow, Knighton is approached via the A4113 . Clun is on the A488 six miles to the north.*

* *Knighton Information Centre is also the information centre for Offa's Dyke. Its address is West Street, Knighton, LD7 1EW. Tel. 01547 528753. Knighton is the centre for exploring Offa's Dyke and running north The Clun Forest has the most complete section.*

Clun – still quiet

The Heart of Housman's Country

Wenlock Edge and Corvedale

North of Ludlow the broad fertile valley of Corvedale runs between Wenlock Edge and Brown Clee. Its soils are red and its houses of yellow-grey stone.

Wenlock Edge is an escarpment that extends fifteen miles from Craven Arms to Much Wenlock. Its north-west face is steep and prominent and its line is long and straight. The south-east side is a gentle slope into Corvedale. The rock of Wenlock Edge is Silurian limestone, full of fossils of marine life. It has been quarried for hundreds of years and it is still quarried. A.E.H. wrote 'On Wenlock Edge the wood's in trouble', (ASL XXXI), ; it is wooded for most of its length.

*   *The National Trust owns about 7 miles of of Wenlock Edge. There are various public and permitted paths traversing it. The National Trust has a leaflet about these.*

Brown Clee

Brown Clee lies a few miles north of its partner **Titterstone Clee**. Geologically they are similar, of sandstone with a flatish top because of the dhustone cap. There are two domes to Brown Clee. The one to the north is called Abdon Burf. This is the highest at 1790 feet. It is here the beacon burned for Queen Victoria (ASL I) and has burned on many occasions before and since. To the south is Clee Burf, 1650 feet.

Brown Clee has some woodland but most of it is open moorland with heather cover - England's southern-most grouse moor. Around the hill are villages and hamlets, which long ago used to house the miners who worked in the quarries and ironworkings, and farms which used to use the hill as common grazing.

One of the villages was, Abdon. Was, because Abdon is much reduced in size and is now a scatter of houses and an isolated church in a circular churchyard. In earlier times there were many more houses and an iron forge. There are traces of the abandoned village in the fields.

When lads were home from labour
   At Abdon under Clee,
A man would call his neighbour
   And both would send for me.
And where the light in lances
   Across the mead was laid,
There to the dances
   I fetched my flute and played.

Pages 112 & 113
Corvedale from Nordy Bank.
Looking towards the eastern slope of
Wenlock Edge and beyond

The youth toward his fancy
   Would turn his brow of tan,
And Tom would pair with Nancy
   And Dick step off with Fan;
The girl would lift her glances
   To his, and both be mute;
Well went the dances
   At evening to the flute.

Two verses of LP XLI

A.E.H. later admitted his reference to Abdon was not accurate so he
probably never saw a dance there.
There were however just about
enough inhabitants at the time to hold
a dance. Perhaps he need not have
made the admission.

Another verse, from the same poem
is particularly interesting as well as
delightful.

Wenlock Edge was umbered,
   And bright was Abdon Burf,
And warm between them
      slumbered
   The smooth green miles of turf;
Until from grass and clover
   The upshot beam would fade,
And England over
   Advanced the lofty shade.

A.E.H. describes how the sun
sinking below Wenlock Edge can
catch the top of Brown Clee with an
'upshot' beam. It is hard to believe
that anyone would write this verse
without having seen the phenome-
non, and it is evidence that he knew a
little more of Shropshire than he
troubled to tell .

*It is worth exploring Brown Clee and
Corvedale. The lanes are narrow and you*
really need a good map.

*   One very good vantage point is Nordy
Bank. Here on the western slope of Brown
Clee is an ancient British earthwork fort
which is interesting enough in its own
right but it also makes an excellent point
to see the sweep of Corvedale and the
slope of Wenlock, and it is a good starting
point to walk up Brown Clee. There is
parking for cars. The grid reference is
573847*

Hughley

Hughley, A.E.H. did not know. He
wrote ASL LXI without having been
to there, choosing it because he liked
the name.

Hughley Steeple

The vane on Hughley steeple
   Veers bright, a far-known sign,
And there lie Hughley people,
   And there lie friends of mine.
Tall in their midst the tower
   Divides the shade and sun,
And the clock strikes the hour
   And tells the time to none.

From ASL LXI

The village church actually has a
small timbered belfry - not a steeple.
The poem goes on to describe how
the suicides are buried to the north of
the steeple, which is not true of
Hughley either. The poem is surely a
composite. Perhaps A.E.H. had the
steeple of St John's, Bromsgrove, in
mind, but the suicides to the north

must have been elsewhere. Incidentally there are few steeples in Shropshire most of its churches have towers.

Hughley is below the scarp of Wenlock Edge four miles from Much Wenlock.

Much Wenlock

The town of Much Wenlock is right at the north-easterly end of the Wenlock Edge. There is one poem in which it features, ASL XXXIX.

'Tis time ,I think, by Wenlock town
    The golden broom should blow;
The hawthorn sprinkled up and
        down
    Should charge the land with snow.

Although A.E.H. said he knew Wenlock (he might have meant the Edge rather than the town), his notebooks show that this poem was first written about Stourbridge, a town a few miles north of Bromsgrove. (Stourbridge is not noted for broom - he might have really been thinking of Kinver Edge, an area of heathland near Stourbridge). Much Wenlock has a narrow mainstreet, off the A458 between Shrewsbury and Bridgnorth. The close-packed houses are of various periods and interesting in their variety. Near to the town are the very impressive ruins of the seventh century Wenlock Priory, once a very prosperous monastery.

Much Wenlock is between Shrewsbury and Bridgnorth on the A458.

Hughley church – and its belfry

Much Wenlock's Information Centre is in the centre of the town It is open from April to October. The address is: The Guildhall, Much Wenlock. Tel: 01952 727679. It is the best source of information about the town and Wenlock Edge. In the same building is a museum with features on the geology of the Edge and the history of the town.

* The Priory is a remarkable ruin of what must have been a large and magnificent building before the Reformation.

It is an English Heritage property , open daily April-September, 10.00 am-6.00 pm, and for the rest of the year Wednesday-Sunday 10.00 am-4.00 pm. Tel. 01952 727466.

And the North of Housman's Country

Shrewsbury

In ASL XXVIII A.E.H. aptly describes Shrewsbury; its old town standing on a sandstone outcrop high above the Severn and set in a loop of the river which nearly makes it an island .

High the vanes of Shrewsbury gleam
Islanded in Severn stream;
The bridges from the steepled crest
Cross the water east and west.

And its English and Welsh bridges are just as described. It is a unique setting for a town and the town is as interesting as its setting. The rest of this poem shows that A.E.H. was conscious of the historic role of Shrewsbury at a pivotal border position in the struggle between Celtic British and Anglo-Saxons, as it later was between the Welsh and Normans.

The flag of morn in conqueror's state
Enters at the English gate:
The vanquished eve, as night prevails,
Bleeds upon the road to Wales.

Today the town shows strong evidence of its prosperity in Tudor times when wool merchants poured their wealth into fine half-timbered houses. The Georgian and Victorian periods left their mark too with some fine buildings.

The railway builders managed to cross the neck of the loop in the

Severn bringing the station close into the town; some of the station is actually over the river. Looking down on the station is the jail, its barred windows peeping over high brick walls. Again A.E.H. describes it truly. The trains do groan as they negotiate the curve below.

They hang us now in Shrewsbury jail:
    The whistles blow forlorn,
And trains all night groan on the rail
    To men that die at morn.

There sleeps in Shrewsbury jail to-
        night,
    Or wakes, as may betide,
A better lad, if things went right,
    Than most that sleep outside.
                        From ASL IX

There is a red sandstone castle which the Normans built . It is the home of the Shropshire Regimental Museum. A.E.H. knew something of the history of the King's Shropshire Light Infantry, which did serve on the Nile in the nineteenth century.

It dawns in Asia, tombstones show
    And Shropshire names are read;
And the Nile spills his overflow
    Beside the Severn's dead.
                        From ASL I

Shrewsbury is 25 miles north of Ludlow on the A49. This road running

Shrewsbury
Islanded in Severn stream

*north and south through Shropshire gives
a good overview of the Housman's
Country. Travelling north to wards
Shrewsbury from Craven Arms there are
views of the wooded scarp of Wenlock
Edge on the right before passing the big
bare humps of Long Mynd on the left .
Then on the right there are the hills of
Caer Caradoc with rocks breaking
through the surface and after that the
country opens out into the plain of north
Shropshire with Shrewsbury in this
setting.*

* *The address of the Shrewsbury Tourist
Information Centre is Music Hall, The
Square, SY1 1LH. Tel. 01743 350761.
There is much to see in Shrewsbury and
it is a good centre for the north of
Housman's Country.*

Wroxeter (Viroconium)

Wroxeter is the modern name for
the Roman town of Viroconium and
Uriconium was the name the British
gave it. A.E.H. shortened it with
poetic license to Uricon. As a Latin
scholar he would find the traces of
Roman occupation of Britain especially interesting. He shows his
sympathy with the Roman.

On Wenlock Edge the wood's in
    trouble;
  His forest fleece the Wrekin heaves;
The gale, it plies the saplings double,
  And thick on Severn snow the
    leaves.

'Twould blow like this through holt
    and hanger
  When Uricon the city stood:
'Tis the old wind in the old anger,
  But then it threshed another wood.

Then 'twas before my time, the
    Roman
  At yonder heaving hill would stare:
The blood that warms an English
    yeoman,
  The thoughts that hurt him, they
    were there.

There, like the wind through woods
    in riot,
  Through him the gale of life blew
    high;
The tree of man was never quiet:
  Then'twas the Roman, now 'tis I.

The gale, it plies the saplings double,
  It blows so hard, 'twill soon be
    gone:
To-day the Roman and his trouble
  Are ashes under Uricon.

               ASL XXXI

Viroconium was an important
Roman town; the fourth largest in
Britain. Its garrison was key to con-
trolling the Welsh border. A.E.H. may
have visited the excavations that were
taking place in 1894.

* *Wroxeter is five miles south-east from
Shrewsbury on the B4380. It is on flat
land beside the Severn and the Romans
would feel at the frontier as they looked
across the plain towards Wales.*

* *The Roman site belongs to English
Heritage. The centrepiece of the ruins is*

the bath complex.

It is open daily from April to October, 10.00 am-6.00 pm and Wednesday-Sunday, 10.00 am-4.00 pm the rest of the year. Tel: 01743 761330

The Wrekin

Close to Uriconium the Wrekin rises in a great dome-shape from Severn plain. A.E.H. wrote 'his forest fleece the Wrekin heaves'. It is well wooded too. It is not the highest hill in Shropshire by any means but its isolation makes it imposing. Its height is 1335ft.

The volcanic Precambrian rocks of which it is composed are very old like those of Long Mynd and the Stretton Hills. There was an iron age fort on the top from which the British Cornovii defended their territory against the Romans before they integrated and joined them in Viroconium. It has always been a key landmark and the site for beacons.

** There are walks up the Wrekin. For information - tourist information centres at **Shrewsbury** and **Ironbridge.***

Severn Shore

Buildwas

The Severn winds on southeasterly in great curls through the last of the flat land towards wooded hills. Before it enters the Severn Gorge it passes near the village of Buildwas. Buildwas, as mentioned earlier, was sustituted by A.E.H. in ASL XXVIII for Bewdley as the place downstream from Shrew-

bury to which the Severn ran 'Coloured with the death of man'. Probably this was in the process of adding further Shropshire identity to his poems when the title *A Shropshire Lad* had been adopted.

Away from the village, by the banks of the Severn, among trees are the ruins of the 12th century Buildwas Abbey with solid columns and Romanesque arches. The monks of Buildwas once forged iron and paved the way for the the industry that developed at Ironbridge.

* Buildwas is on the B4380.

* The Abbey is approached from the A4169. It is an English Heritage property, open April-September. Tel. 01952 433274.

* Viroconium, the Wrekin & Buildwas are close to Attingham Park, an 18th century mansion in Repton grounds – the regional headquarters of the National Trust, which has a number of other properties in Housman's Country, including much of Wenlock Edge. Tel. 01743 709203.

The Severn Gorge

In geological time the Severn, which had once flowed north did the seemingly impossible and cut its way into the hills which flank the Severn Gorge. The entrance is now marked by the cooling towers of a power station sending white plumes of vapour billowing into the sky. At the top of the gorge is Ironbridge, once blackened by the iron industry which started the Industrial Revolution. A.E.H. certainly never wrote about Ironbridge. In his time it would be at the height of its industry, and sooty and grim.

The Severn slides on to Broseley and deep in its cutting, in five miles, to Bridgnorth.

* *The Ironbridge Musem is now a major tourist attraction. It is open daily throughout the year. Hours vary but are based on 10.00 am to 5.00 pm. Tel. 01952 433522.*

* *There is a tourist information centre at Ironbridge.*
Address; The Wharfage, Ironbridge, Telford, IF8 7AW. Tel. 01952 432166

Bridgnorth from the south

Bridgnorth

The main part of Bridgnorth, the High Town is set dramatically on a high cliff over the Severn with steps, and a cliff railway down to the Low Town and the river. The town is capped with the ruins of a Norman castle, leaning at an impossible angle after the Royalists destroyed it in the Civil War, and also by a fine neoclassical church designed by Thomas Telford.

There are wonderful views of the Severn with its meadows and wooded banks as it flows on south.

Housman visited Bridgnorth when he was gathering local colour. He remembered his mother telling him about the steps to the church. He might have been just in time to see

the last sailing barge. He probably travelled on the Severn Valley Railway.

The Severn south of Bridgnorth

* *Bridgnorth Tourist Information Centre is in Listley Street, Bridgnorth, Shropshire, WV16 4AW. Tel: 01746 763358.*

On to Bewdley

The last stretch of the Severn in Housman's Country, from Bridgnorth to Bewdley, is what A.E.H. would think of most as Severn shore. After some open pastures south of Bridg-north the river runs swiftly through the gorge, with pastures and woods high above it. Now that attempts at industry have gone it is a quiet landscape with harmonious names like Arley, Highley and Hampton Loade.

* *This part of the Severn is made accessible by the Severn Valley Railway. (see* **Bewdley***)*

Bredon

Bredon, the setting for a lovely tragic much-set-to-music poem, is not in Shropshire but in Worcestershire.

In summertime on Bredon
  The bells they sound so clear;
Round both the shires they ring them
  In steeples far and near,
  A happy noise to hear.

Here of a Sunday morning
  My love and I would lie,
And see the coloured counties,
  And hear the larks so high
  About us in the sky.

                from ASL XXI

Bredon Hill was one of the hills that that A.E.H. could see, blue in the distance twenty miles from Fockbury, to the south in that great panorama from Mount Pisgah (**Housman's Hill**). He wrote the poem before ASL was put together with a Shropshire theme.

Bredon Hill is a long whaleback of a hill. It is geologically a limestone outlier of the Cotwolds much of it cultivated or pasture. It is surrounded by villages with churches, though most of them ,with the exception of Bredon village, have towers rather than spires. It is close to the border of Worcestershire and Gloucestershire and for the views of the counties with their patchwork of fields 'Coloured' is an apt word. A.E.H. worked hard selecting it.

Some people have tried to suggest that A.E.H really meant the poem to be about The Breidden Hills which are in Montgomeryshire but there is little doubt that that he meant Bredon and he felt sufficiently attached to the poem to put it into ASL without alteration.

For A.E.H., as a boy in Bromsgrove, Bredon was on the rail route to Woodchester via Cheltenham. Whether he alighted there and climbed the hill we do not know, but it seems likely.

* *Bredon is near Junction 9 on the M5 and between Tewkesbury and Evesham.*

* *There are walks up the hill and round Bredon. The nearest information centre is at Tewkesbury. Tel. 01684 295027.*

Acknowledgements

Text

The author would like to thank the many people who have helped with this book. Some of those who have contributed most are recorded here.

For overall help and advice:
Mr Dieter Baer, Mr J. Roy Birch, Mr Jeremy Bourne, Mr Alan Holden, Mr Joe Hunt, Mrs Jennie McGregor-Smith, Mr Jim Page, Mr Stephen Page, Mr John Pugh.

For help with sections of the book as listed:
Bromsgrove
General, John Pugh, Dr Alan Richards; Christ Church, Catshill,   Rev. Andrew Vessey; The Clock House, Mr John Sleigh; Housmans, The late Mr B. Bellingham and Mrs B. Bellingham; Perry Hall, the Management;   St John's Church, Canon John Davies; Bromsgrove School, Mr T. Taylor, Mr Jeremy Bourne; The Lower House, Mr Raybould.
Oxford
St. John's College, Mr Nicholas Purcell , Ms Angela Williams; General, Mr Keith Jebb; Epwell Mill, Mr Rupert Withers and Mrs Audrey Kennett; Souldern Court, Mr Christopher Hodgson.
London
The Patent Office, Mr James Harrison, Mr John Hewish, The staff of the British Library, Science and Information Service; Highgate, Mr Sidney Tobin; The British Museum, Mr Christopher Date; University College London, Mr Ian W. G. Martin, Ms Susan Trubshaw.
Cambridge
Trinity College, Mr A. P. Simm, Dr D. McKitterick. Mrs L. Dench.
Woodchester
Mrs Doreen Crawford (including access to records by her late husband, Mr Neville Crawford).
Bath
Mr Basil Greenslade
Shropshire
General, Mrs Jane Caulcott.

For permission to quote from material which is copyright:
Poems and extracts from A.E.H.'s *Collected Poems* and extracts from writings of Laurence Housman- Random House UK Limited.
Extract from *A.E.Housman*, Grant Richards - Oxford University Press.
Extract from an article in The Housman Society Journal Number 1 - Rt Hon J. Enoch Powell

For all other material quoted every reasonable effort has been made to trace copyright. Thanks are due to the Society of Authors for their help.

Illustrations

The author is indebted to the following for kind permission to reproduce illustrations:
'Housman and I' (Cover) - Mr David Birtwhistle
A.E.H. (Title page) - Mr Gerald Symons
A.E.H. by Francis Dodd (Page 10) - The President & Fellows of St John's College, Oxford
Bromsgrove in the 1880s. Part of a larger drawing (Page 14) - Mr Norman Neasom, Dr Alan Richards and the Bromsgrove Society
Housman family photographs, The Rev Thomas Housman (Page 23), Edward Housman (Page 26), Sarah Jane Housman (Page 27), Alfred and Robert (Page 39), A.E.H. at 18 (Page 49), - Mr John Pugh.
The Clock House (Page 29) - Mr Gerald Symons
The Clock House (Page 30) - Mr R. J. Richardson

The last days of the Clock House (Page 31) - The Bromsgrove Messenger
St Giles (Page 54) - The Francis Frith Collection
Fleet Street about 1890 (Pages 58/59) - Keeper of Prints and Maps, Guildhall Library, London
The old Patent Office (Page 61) - The British Library Science Reference and Information Service
Moses and Adalbert Jackson (Page 65) - Mrs Doreen Crawford
The Graeco- Roman Salon, the British Museum (Page 70) - The British Museum
University College London (Page 73) - University College London
Cambridge College rooftops (Pages 78/79) - Mr Tim Rawle
The Great Gate, Trinity College (Pages 81) - Trinity College Library
Autograph from Last Poems (Page 85) - The Syndics of the Fitzwilliam Museum, Cambridge.
Petty Cury, about 1920 (Page 87) - The Cambridgeshire Collection, Cambridgeshire Libraries.
The Butter Cross, Ludlow (Page 108) - Shropshire Museum Services
Clun (Page 111)- Molineux Associates
Shrewsbury (Page 118) - Mr Walter Hopewell
Bridgnorth (Page 121) - Bridgnorth District Council
The Severn (Page 122) - Bridgnorth District Council

All other drawings, maps and photographs, except those of old Bromsgrove on pages 16 and 17, are by the author.

Bibliography

Many books have been consulted in putting together Housman's Places. The following have been most useful with regard to the life of A.E.H.:

A. E. Housman: *The Scholar-Poet*, by Richard Perceval Graves, (Routledge & Kegan Paul 1979). A very full and good general biography. Unfortunately out of print.

A. E. Housman: *A Critical Biography*, Macmillan 1983). Lives up to its title. Less detailed a biography than Graves'.

Bromsgrove and the Housmans, by John Pugh, (The Housman Society 1974). Packed with information about the family and Bromsgrove.

A. E. Housman, *A Sketch*, by A. S. F. Gow (Cambridge University Press 1936). The first biographical book about A.E.H.. Gow knew him at Cambridge.

A.E.H. by Laurence Housman, (Jonathan Cape 1937). A brother's view.

The Unexpected Years, by Laurence Housman (Jonathan Cape 1937). Insights into A.E.H.'s early family life.

Housman 1897-1936, by Grant Richards, (Oxford University Press 1941). An account of their business relationship and friendship.

A Buried Life, by Percy Withers, 1940. Full of anecdotes.

A. E. Housman by Keith Jebb (Seren Books 1992). Some interesting essays.

Housman's Poems by John Bayley, (Clarendon Press 1992). The most recent academic analysis of A.E.H.'s poems.

The Letters of A. E. Housman, edited by Henry Maas, (Rupert Hart-Davis 1971).

The Special Edition of *The Bromsgrovian*, the magazine of Bromsgrove School 1936. Essays by Laurence Housman, Kathleen Symons, A.W. Pollard, A.S.F. Gow. and others

A.E.Housman: Collected Poems and Selected Prose edited by Christopher Ricks (Allen Lane, The Penguin Group 1988). The most complete edition of A.E.H.'s writings to date.

Index

This index is selective, not comprehensive, mainly identifying the most important places and people relevant to to A.E.H. and his works. References to chapters and sections are in bold type; to illustrations in italics.

The Housman Society

The Housman Society (Registered Charity number 1001107) was founded in 1973. The primary objects of the Society are to promote knowledge and appreciation of the lives and works of A. E. Housman and other members of his family, to encourage research and writing about the family, and to promote the cause of literature and poetry among the public. The Society is based in Bromsgrove and has members worldwide. There is a branch in Ludlow and also branches in the USA and Japan. It produces an annual Journal which aims to publish critical researches, documentary evidence and book reviews. It organises programmes of activities including, lectures, discussions, poetry readings, and commemorations in Bromsgrove and Ludlow.

For further information contact: The Secretary, 80 New Road, Bromsgrove, B60 2LA.